Land Army Days
CINDERELLAS OF THE SOIL

by Knighton Joyce

AURORA
PUBLISHING

© AURORA PUBLISHING

ISBN: 1 85926 032 2

Distributed by: Aurora Enterprises Ltd.
                     Unit 9C, Bradley Fold Trading Estate,
                     Radcliffe Moor Road,
                     Bradley Fold,
                     BOLTON BL2 6RT
                     Tel: 0204 370753/2
                     Fax: 0204 370751

Edited by: Knighton Joyce

Printed
and bound by: Manchester Free Press,
                     Unit E3, Longford Trading Estate,
                     Thomas Street,
                     Stretford,
                     Manchester M32 0JT.

Front cover: The end of a working day

CONTENTS

*T*his book is dedicated

to those who also served,

The Women's Land Army.

ACKNOWLEDGEMENTS

I want to say a great big thank you to everyone who helped me with information and advice, especially ex-members of

The Women's Land Army for taking the time out to sit down, put pen to paper, and tell me their stories which made such enjoyable reading. I must also offer my heartfelt thanks for trusting me with their very precious photographs.

I shall be forever grateful to Carol Woodhead for her typing skills and enduring patience whilst trying to read my untidy scribble.

My thanks to the ladies of Bridlington Stationers who showed such interest in my project when it was just a seed.

To the memory of the late Mrs Norma Best, a great lady, who gave me encouragement when I needed it most. I shall miss her always.

Lastly to Mrs Brenda Goldthorpe, ex W.L.A.,
for giving me the idea.

INTRODUCTION

The Womens Land Army consisted of girls from every walk of life; from the slums of Liverpool to a Yorkshire miner's daughter, from an only child born with a silver spoon in her mouth to a counter assistant in a high class store in London.

At first, it was a life of gruelling hard toil and monotony, in all weathers despite what the glamorous posters had depicted! Most felt home-sick, cried themselves to sleep at night, and wondered what on earth had possessed them to condemn themselves to such a miserable existence. Cold, wet feet, frost-bitten fingers in winter, aching backs, overcoats that let in the driving rain, sleet and snow; small amounts of war rationed food (beetroot sandwiches being the most hated of all).

Work involved trimming hedges, cleaning out ditches, dung spreading, threshing, raking, harrowing, ploughing, even rick building and thatching. The caring of one's machinery was a must; a job that every Land Girl had to be able to do. The farm horse always had careful grooming; dairy milking by hand was a chore that had to be mastered, as was a knowledge of crop pests, weed control, soil types, animal diseases, calf rearing and glass-house work; the list was endless.

Harvesting time came around and the Land Girl was surprised at her sheer physical strength and powers of endurance as she mastered loading the sheaves. Dealing with moody animals and bad-tempered farmers who were never satisfied at a job well done because she, the Land Girl, a mere woman, had done it. All the while she was gaining valuable experience that she was going to remember and put to good use in later life; learning about human nature, making life-long friends with girls she had grown to like, admire and trust because they were all part of a valuable team, working together in harmony, singing, laughing and sometimes crying over the death of a loved one that the war had taken from them. They carried on with a cheerful smile, these Cinderellas of the Soil, knowing the job had to be done.

However, it was not all work and no play for the Land Girl and she looked forward to her time off as she would in Civvy Street.

The black-out is in force and the night tar black as the Land Girls set off with a few shillings spending money in their pockets. Mounting their bikes and setting off amid giggles whilst wobbling and weaving their way up and down the country lanes and trying to keep sight of the person in front - an almost impossible task as only two of the bikes carried a lamp; the one in front and the one bringing up the rear. Once in the village, the girls enjoy a sing-song round a piano in the local pub, a glass of cider, then over the road to the old church hall for a couple of hours, dancing to records of the best swing bands of the day. The lads are waiting to swing the girls off their feet in a quick-step, hold them close in a waltz; lads wearing the uniforms of the Army, Navy and Air Force.

Then one day the Yanks appear, larger than life and twice as smart. They breeze into the English way of life, eager to show a girl a good time, showering them with nylons, chocolate and gum, but most of all with mouth-watering food. After beetroot sandwiches, G.I. food was a luxury not to be missed.

Jitterbugging was the order of the day and most girls were eager to be taught. The G.I.s had swing bands brought over from the States, the legendary Glenn Miller being the most prominent. The G.I.s were hard to overlook, and for the most part the great British public made them welcome; after all, they were some mothers' sons, and were fighting our war alongside our boys. Young, good-natured and romantic, often home-sick, they drank hard liquor, rolled their eyes at a pretty girl and found it hard to understand the English and their country ways. When the war was over, they took English brides back with them, some to live happily ever after, but most doomed to failure.

The Land Girls lived up to expectation, much to the amazement and growing admiration of the farmers they worked for. Working in the shadow of the flag for very little pay, they considered it their duty; a duty filled with true loyalty to the crown and country. It was their assignment, and they carried it out with pride, emerging as the "Unsung Heroines" of the war, but knowing that they could always walk tall because they, the Land Girls, would always be a part of English history and, I am sure, will never be forgotten by those who also served.

Yes, the Land Girl put together a work force second to none, a force to be admired, unequalled during its reign, accomplishing much through the long, tough, toiling days in the fields.

FOREWORD

The Women's Land Army, often called "The Forgotten Army", was formed in 1917 by Mr Roland Prothero, the then Minister of Agriculture. The Great War began in 1914 and after three years, food supplies were so low that a new organisation, namely the Women's Land Army, was formed.

The so-called great war ended in 1918, but in June 1939 thousands of trained W.L.A. members were sent into employment, ready to give their all for King and Country when Britain went to war with Germany.

The W.L.A. was part of the Ministry of Agriculture and run entirely by women, the Honorary Director being Lady Denman, O.B.E., who gave her own home, Balcombe Place, for the W.L.A. headquarters.

The W.L.A. was extremely well organised and recruiting suitable girls depended upon agreement with the War Cabinet, Ministry of Labour, The National Farmers Union and the National Union of Agricultural Workers. The Agricultural Wages Board dealt with all wages. Annual estimates had to be submitted to the Treasury, including costs of training, uniform supplies, hostel and travelling expenses. The requisitioning of Land Army hostels was dealt with by the Ministry of Labour and Works.

Counties had to be organised separately, and each county had its Organising Secretary Committee and Local Representative. The job of the Representative was a very detailed one, requiring a great deal of tact. A girl who had to adjust quickly to life on the land could have no end of troubles (bad behaviour, erratic love life, health, and resentments to name but some) and the poor harassed Rep had to discipline, persuade, warn and comfort each girl in her numerous troubles, feel and express relief at her happiness and contentment in her work, and remember that the Land Girls were employed by individual farmers, and not by the State. At the end of the day the Rep was acting on behalf of The County Office, and it was The County Secretary who saw that all conditions of employment were met, the Land Army not being subject to military discipline.

The Land Army uniform, though not stylish, was very smart if worn with a good posture, and consisted of brown breeches, green jersey, pale Aertex shirt, fawn overcoat and black gum-boots. Hats were worn at a jaunty angle (more often than not) at the back of the head. Dungarees were also provided, along with hob- nailed boots, wellingtons, so'wester and oilskins.

In the many letters I received most of the W.L.A. girls wonder why they are never mentioned at the memorial service at the Cenotaph in November. I took it upon myself to write to Her Majesty and ask why the Land Girls were overlooked. In November 1991, the Women's Land Army was named as part of the War effort for the very first time, before Her Majesty Queen Elizabeth II.

Knighton Joyce

Chapter 1

LAND GIRLS AT WORK

We met on the Midland Station,
In Nineteen forty two.
All were young and carefree,
We were off to pastures new.

Twenty two young ladies
Were off to work the land.
All in spruce new uniforms,
Complete with green arm bands.

Down we went to Beaulieu,
To the house of Lady Dent.
You see, for her War effort,
This lovely house she'd lent.

We toiled in wet, cold winters
And in summer's searing heat.
Often we had backache,
Or tender, swollen feet.

But we made the best of it
In spite of the poor grub.
And had a bit of fun at night,
Down at the local pub.

Many years have passed along,
Since those Wartime years.
We tend to forget the problems,
Hard work, poor pay and fears.

We remember all the good things,
The laughter and the fun.
Village 'Hops' and dancing,
When the long hard day was done.

Now in Nineteen eighty nine,
A few of us have lunch.
We reminisce, laugh and talk
While we sit and munch.

Sadly our numbers have dwindled,
But we have some memories to treasure.
So when we meet at the 'Royal'
We sit and talk at leisure.

Edna Keena
Nottingham

LAND GIRLS AT WORK

I became a Land Girl in 1943 and have never regretted it. I loved the life and have always considered that the W.L.A. taught me a lot about the land, life and human nature. I took to it like a duck takes to water. After living and working in war-torn London, to be in the country was like being born again after the heart-rending senseless destruction I had seen back home.

As I worked the fields in Suffolk I met girls from every walk of life who, like myself, had experienced what the War really meant. To us, it was a whole new life and I for one never wanted it to end. I glowed with a special inner radiance that the love of the country brought out in me. The hard work got rid of all the surplus pounds I had carried around for the last couple of years, and for the first time that I could remember I had a spot-free face. I was twenty years old and had discovered a whole new ball game.

I had worked in a large London store and going home one day, found my house and half the street gone after a bomb attack. My house was just a shell. I had lost everything, including my dear Mum and Dad. Showing the stiff upper lip that we Londoners were famous for, I knew that life had to go on and took up the offer of a friend to live with her and her family until I sorted my life out.

I had seen posters depicting healthy rosy-cheeked Land Girls with a cute little lamb tucked under each arm, and suddenly thought "Why not?" It would get me out of London. Not giving a thought to the hard work entailed, and not knowing one end of a cow from another, I signed on and remember thinking "In for a penny, in for a pound". Thousands of girls had joined and had done their training, be it scant or not, and so would I. Not being stupid by any means, I soon realised that it took brawn (an awful lot of it) as well as brain.

After the three weeks so-called training period, I was sent to a small farm and told to help with all general farm duties. Nothing specific, but just to use my common sense. If I could see anything that wanted doing, just get on with it. The farmer had neglected to tell me that my day would start at 7 am and finish at 8 or 9 pm, with only half an hour for lunch and maybe a quick tea break in the afternoon, if I was lucky. It was high summer at this time, and every hour was spent in and around the farm, in the fields, and anywhere else that I was needed. My white, tender hands were a thing of the past. Instead they became rough and calloused, with my once long nails cut short and minus nail polish. Never having had back ache in my life, I now suffered a never ending pain in the small of the back, and rolled into bed at the end of the day to lay like a stone statue not daring to move in case the pounding pain transferred itself all around my aching body. Of course this did not last forever. My limbs soon became used to the heavy manual labour and my body became one with my brain, which was always alert.

Life could also be very funny. The farmer was

a good mimic and had me rolling about in helpless laughter at his satirical take-off of Frank Randall and Old Mother Riley. Sadly, I was moved on up to Yorkshire, just outside Skipton, and I really missed the many laughs I had with that farmer.

The countryside around Skipton was absolutely beautiful, with air so pure and sweet-smelling, a positive delight after the smoke of London, and I felt my heart lift on the first sight of the hills and dales of this part of Yorkshire. It made one feel that the war was really worth fighting, when you beheld beauty such as that.

I did not live on a farm this time, but was in a hostel with sixteen other girls. I really liked hostel life, but we didn't get enough to eat. Beetroot seemed to be the only thing that was plentiful, and to this day I shudder at the sight of beetroot. I got along very well with the other girls, but at the end of a hard day we were too tired to be good company for each other at night, and would just tumble into bed, asleep almost before our heads touched the pillow.

We were sent out daily to the farms, which were mostly cattle farms, so of course we had to give a hand with the milking. I had been taught how to milk, but had really never liked the job because deep down I was nervous of the large, cumbersome beasts. On my first day, I approached the animal with thudding heart and tried to talk calmly to the poor, unfortunate cow that had to put up with my heavy, clumsy fingers pulling and squeezing her teats as if they were made of elastic. It was several

weeks before I really mastered the art, and found that if I sang to the cows we got along fine. They seemed to like my soprano voice and would stand quietly swishing their tails whilst I got on with the job of relieving them of their rich creamy milk. When the farmer came upon me singing my head off, he would pretend to stuff his ears with cotton wool, slap me on the back, tell me that I was a "rum-un" and go away laughing his head off.

I shall never forget my first sight of the farm bull mounting the cow. It took all my self control not to run post haste back to stricken London.

I must confess that I found the field work heavy going, but never let it get me down. Working in the rain was not pleasant. The water always seemed to find a way of trickling down our necks, so we would tie a sack around our shoulders and carry on regardless. The Land Girl had a lot to put up with - bad weather conditions, poor food, jealous and distrustful farmers' wives, and envious local village girls, all of which we learned to cope with, not to mention our hostel warden/housekeeper.

After four happy months at Skipton I moved on down to Kent. I had visited Kent before the war, so knew the layout of the county which is quite pretty. This time I was in a hostel with twenty girls and a rip-roaring housekeeper who had a Jekyll and Hyde character, no personality, was bordering on the eccentric, and was so cross-eyed, one wondered how she managed to walk in a straight line. One of the girls gave her the nickname

"Whichway" which suited her down to the ground, the reason being while in the process of telling one of us off in no uncertain terms, she had the uncanny ability of being able to look at the miscreant with one eye and at the same time fix the other one on a girl on the other side of the room who would be in fits of hysterics at this extraordinary feat. The woman was a misanthrope, who loved to belittle us any chance she got, insisted that we were a common, uncouth, lazy lot of ungrateful little brats, and proceeded to go out of her way to make life as uncomfortable for us as she could. However, we put up with her bad temper, ignored her most of the time, and came to the conclusion that she was entitled to her own opinion, be it right or wrong.

The girls were a good bunch, Mavis from South Yorkshire was a good friend and her down to earth humour kept me entertained when the heavens opened and we worked ankle deep in mud.

We did get time off and would go dancing, seeking out the dance halls or going to the village hops. These were always well attended as the small villages did not have much in the way of entertainment. The local girls would glare at the Land Girls when the local lads asked us to dance. We wore our uniforms most of the time. We could not afford to buy clothes on the pay we got and, in any case, clothing coupons were few and far between.

I loved to be on the dance floor. It was one of the few pleasures in life that we over-worked Land Girls got. Mavis and I went to Norwich one weekend to stay with her sister. It was a weekend I shall remember always as one of the best of my life. She took us dancing to the G.I. base. What a super band they had and what nice fellows I found the G.I.s to be. They were lovable rogues, great talkers, even greater dancers, called everyone honey or sweetheart, and really knew how to enjoy themselves. They were also as smart as paint and the ones I met treated me like the lady I hope I was. To finish the night off, a G.I. called Newton asked me to dance with him in the Jitterbug contest. To my delight, we won and I got six pairs of nylons which, in those days, were like gold dust. When we were announced as the winners, Newton said to me "Gee, honey, you may do a man's job but you sure don't Jitterbug like one". He also told me that the Land Girls were greatly admired by the G.I.s for the job they did on the land, and that we should have a medal at the end of the war. I remember how proud I felt at his words, and was to remember them once again when the war was over and we came out with nothing for all our efforts.

I remember that white and coloured G.I.s did not mix at dances, and we were not allowed to dance with the black G.I.s, which I thought was so ridiculous when they stood side by side during battle. It was a cruel segregation..

The G.I. parties with their mouth watering food are legendary. In food-rationed Britain, one could only dream of such goodies. On being told to "Weigh in, honey", we did just that, even stuffing bits and pieces into our handbags in order to have another feast back at the hostel.

We had some of the most heart-rending songs during the war. Even now, when I hear "I Haven't said Thanks for that Lovely Weekend", "I'll Be Seeing You" and "The London I Love", I could weep buckets for times long gone, even though we were at war.

Our weekend over, back at the hostel the girls would want to know what kind of a time we had and if we had met anyone nice enough to fall in love with. Of course, girls in those days fell in and out of love constantly. During the war a fellow was there one day, and gone the next. If you didn't hear from him again, you were left wondering if he had moved on or had been killed or injured.

We had some very funny, and sometimes embarrassing, moments during our work on the land. One in particular also brings a smile to my face no matter where I happen to be at the time.

Prunes! Shall I ever forget my one and only breakfast of prunes? Our harridan of a housekeeper "Whichway" one morning insisted that we eat the horrible beetle-like things, saying that we didn't have choices in her hostel, get them down us because we'd get nothing else. The horrid things looked absolutely revolting but I forced them down with a shudder, which was not easy to do at 6.30 in the morning. Whichway stood over us grinning like the cat that stole the cream until everyone had eaten and prune stones were spit onto empty plates. As we pulled on our coats and hats, Mavis said

in a loud, carrying voice which was meant to be heard by Whichways "Stuff her and her bloody prunes. Someone should make her eat a bucketful, and I only hope that they would shit her to death". Tilting her hat at a jaunty angle, she marched through the door without waiting to hear the angry reply trembling on Whichway's lips. As we trooped off to walk the mile to the field where we were to spend the day repairing the surrounding hedge (a tough job on the hands), Mavis and I were helpless with laughter at the look on Whichway's face at Mavis's outburst. No doubt even now she would be thinking up a way to get even with us, and we could only hope that it was not another breakfast of prunes.

On reaching the field, we set about our task of repairing the hedge, singing as we worked. Well into the morning, I felt a sharp, stabbing pain in my lower stomach. With a feeling of dread I knew that I had to go to the toilet, and right away. Turning to Mavis, horror struck, I said "Mavis, I have to go to the loo. I feel dreadful and have the most awful stomach ache. What am I going to do, the nearest toilet is a mile away from the farm".

"Only one thing to do", Mavis laughed, "Get your breeches down, a handful of dock leaves, and dive behind the nearest tree".

"I can't", I wailed. "Someone may see me".

"Who's to see you, there's only me here besides the birds, and I don't think the birds will be interested; I know that I'm not", Mavis replied in her down to earth way.

With a large grin, she turned once more to her work. Knowing that I didn't have a choice and getting more desperate by the minute, I raced frantically to the large tree which stood about fifty yards away. Having relieved myself, I straightened my clothing and set my hat firmly on top of my head, starting to realise that the breakfast of prunes were the cause of my down fall, when a gruff male voice from behind me called "Nice bit of rump you have there, girl". I turned to see a pimple-faced youth with large teeth grinning at me. Feeling as if someone had thrown a bucket of ice-cold water over me, I stared at him dumb struck, then started to sweat as I realised that he had seen my naked rear end in all its glory. I could only stand rooted to the spot and if I could have sunk into the ground at his feet, I would have done. As he started to laugh at his own joke, I got the feelingback into my legs and took off at speed to join Mavis who, upon hearing the story, never let me live it down during all our days together in the Land Army.

I could write forever about my Land Girl days and the wonderful companionship I found within the ranks. I have not gone into detail about the jobs we had to do, as most of them have been described in preceding letters. I can only say that two Land Girls were worth four men. Some of the jobs we had to do were hard. It was filthy work in the barns, as most of the dust went into our lungs. Weeding carrots in never-ending rows, cleaning out the ditches, wet cold hands while turnip-picking in dreary fog-filled early mornings, but I would do it all over again if asked. Sadly, we all had to go back to Civvy Street, but I feel the W.L.A. was forgotten too soon; after all, we did our bit and I shall feel everlasting gratitude to Knighton Joyce for bringing us once more to the public's notice. The W.L.A. took its responsibilities seriously - we cared. What a pity the Government of the day did not care enough to give us a gratuity.

A Ivy,
London

I joined the Land Army in September 1940. I swore to serve my King and country. All details being taken, I was then measured for uniform, sworn in, and told that I would be sent for very soon.

In March 1941 I got a letter to say I was to go to Lincolnshire, would be met at Sleaford, and taken to my farm. However, arriving at Sleaford I was told that the farmer wasn't ready for me for another week, so I could go home or to the hostel; so it was to the hostel I went. There were forty four of us and we slept in a big dormitory hut divided into open cubicles of four bunks, with two coke stoves to keep it warm. We were up at

6 am, washed, had breakfast, then detailed off to our farm for the day. Farmers sent transport, or we were given bikes to ride. I was sent to a farm down Horbling Fen about four miles away. We were a little late the first day, and got a dressing down from the farmer (he was a real tartar). We worked at the edge of the field riddling potatoes from clumps. It was cold work and we were only allowed fifteen minutes to eat our packed lunch. The farmer was present much of the day (we hardly got a chance to speak), dressed in leather gaiters and breeches. He carried a short whip with him, and was in the habit of cracking it. He wasn't averse to giving one or another of the farm hands a sharp flip with it if he thought they were slacking. Everyone seemed scared of him, and he was very much hated.

We finished at 5 pm, and on arriving back at the hostel found dinner was over, got another telling off for being late again, and warned not to let it happen tomorrow.
"The farmer wouldn't let us go", we moaned.
"Tell the farmer your contract says that you finish at 4 pm ", we were told.

The next two days followed the same pattern. Meanwhile, we had found out that the farmer had farmed in Africa for years, and treated his workers as slaves, often whipping them. He never used it on us, but if he spoke, he would stand hitting it into his free cupped hand. We were frightened to death of him. On the fourth day, our Supervisor went out to work a day on the farm and to find out what was troubling us. One day was enough for her; she said no girl was going to be treated like that, and the farmer would be struck off with no more Land Girls to help.

My next farm job was a "living in" one. I shared a very small cottage with another girl; no running water, only a hand pump in the garden, and the toilet was just a dry privy in a corner of the wash house. We had a jug of cold water and a bowl in the bedroom. When we had washed, we opened the window and threw the water out.

I didn't like the cold fat bacon so I got bread and jam for breakfast, along with water to drink (I had never drunk tea or coffee in my life). My landlady's name was Mrs Booth. One day I happened to say that I liked bread and dripping. That was it; every day I got one slice, three inches thick with dripping.

I was brought up in a strict home with no swearing or drinking. I soon learned to swear, but never drank.

My work was with the horses. Until I joined the W.L.A. I had never touched a horse in my life, but I soon took to them. Some of them were Shires, others half hunters, but all of them were characters. One was called "Bounce", a big Shire and fairly docile. The waggoner would give me a leg up, and I would straddle the horse while the others sat side saddle. They would make fun of me and shout "Ride 'em cowboy". I took it all in good part, but felt safer sat astride. One day, after the work was done I was sitting on Bounce ready to go home when the planes came hedge-hopping. They did this often, and the horses were frightened half to death. This day Bounce bolted. She threw me forward and I made a grab for the pom on the collar, but instead I got caught by my leather belt which got hooked onto it. I slipped down the side of the horse and hung dangling in mid-air. There were lots of workers going home - the horse was galloping like mad so no-one tried to stop her, just cheered as I went past. I was terrified knowing Bounce wasn't going to stop until she got home. The only thing I could think of was I could be crushed to death against the wall as she went up the narrow passage to her stable. The passage was hardly wide enough to get up with me hanging upside down from her head. However, we made it and she stood in her stall and waited. I was helpless; I couldn't get down, still held by a strong two inch wide leather belt. When the waggoners got back they shouted from the end of the passage "Gladys, are you there? Are you alright?". They told me later that they were frightened to come in and look; they thought the horse had killed me. I was badly shaken on seeing this. The men said they would never laugh at me again for straddling the horse, because if I had been sitting side saddle I would have been killed instantly.

I got a transfer to Yorkshire, near a village called Markington. My farm was about two and a half miles away. It was very hilly country. I had to cross two fields, and go up and down a hill - it was very isolated, with hard work and long hours.

The farmer was a bit of a lad; you had to make sure he never got you on your own in the buildings. His old Dad worked on the farm too. He was actually the tenant, and not the son. He would always try to be around when I was working with the son on my own.

I got friendly with the other girl who worked on the farm. One day she really stunned me when she said that she couldn't read or write. She was a very intelligent girl, but had managed to get by without her parents or fiance knowing. She asked if I would read her letters to her, and write them for her. I was used to writing so took on the job, including writing love letters to her fiance. We kept it our secret and told no-one. However, her fiance was a Catholic and she was changing faith for him, so I advised her to tell the priest - maybe he could help her. I don't know what happened to her, because I got married when my boyfriend was home on leave. We hadn't been married long when my husband was posted to Burma - he was gone for three years.

My next farm was at Oakworth near Skipton. I was in charge of five more Land Girls. There I was, always a good getter-upper, and every morning I woke without an alarm at 6 am; I had all the others up too. It was a proper mixed farm - eleven feet up, cows, sheep, chickens and hens were the main thing. Sheep were the boss's speciality and we didn't have anything to do with them. He had a flock of 250, and used to winter sheep for others. We were on the edge of the moor, two miles from the village. We had two working horses, one that was usually in foal - Molly. When it was time, the boss broke the foals in himself. We reared up to 30,000 chicks a year, from day olds to point of lay.

The boss would never let us handle the bulls in any way. He used to bring the prisoners of war each day from the camp at Skipton to help with hay-time, and when they were allowed to stay with families he took two in to help on the farm. One was very good; he'd worked on farms at home in Germany. He always fed and watered the bulls. On one occasion he saved the boss's life. When he heard a noise from the bull house and went to investigate, the bull had the boss on the floor goring him. He dragged him free, but the boss spent a few weeks in hospital. We all got on with our jobs meanwhile, and the boss was home for Christmas.

One other thing I remember - when we Land Girls were taken short we had to go behind a wall and hope no-one could see us. Long after the war was over and I had settled in the district, it came out that the neighbouring farmer and his wife had a strong pair of binoculars and one day while looking through them saw us Land Girls spending a penny. My, did I blush! There's not much a farmer misses, I can tell you.

Mrs G Beaumont,
Bridlington, Humberside

I was in the W.L.A. approximately four years - a Yorkshire girl, but working in Warwickshire. From working in Schofields' store on hosiery (very up-market then) to working on the land was a huge change! I was sent to Atherstone in Warwickshire, to live in a hostel, which had bemused the local people when it was being built - they thought it was for Italian P.O.W.s.

The local girls hated us, as at the local dances we were popular with local young men! It was a very small town - things certainly heated up when overweight American soldiers came, and were billeted in a huge house close by! Plenty of dances then!

At first, the farmers were reluctant to send to the hostel for us to work on their farms - useless city girls. It didn't take long for them to find out that we were capable of hoeing, etc. Soon we were tractor driving, and I did a lot of that in harvest time. I could also plough a field.

After a while, I went to live in at a farm where I was working a lot - cycling the five miles from the hostel. Going to live in at that farm was a huge mistake, though I stuck it out for more than a year. The old farmer was a widower and had a grown up son at home, plus a housekeeper who hated me. She would have hated any woman living in! She would not give me my food direct - it was passed to the son to pass to me! She also refused to speak to me. When I hurt my back and

DOROTHY NEWTON IN THAT HAT

went to the packing station. I could never understand how a man could be so religious, and yet allow the housekeeper to treat me so badly! On the wireless we were only allowed the news, religious services and farming! I spent hours in my bedroom embroidering by candlelight. In the end, I walked out and got a transfer to a farm near Rugby. The farmer I'd left had four girls after me who did not stay - in the end, the W.L.A. said he could only have girls daily - no more could live in!

To go back to the hostel, we each had a bike - such heavy things, khaki coloured with a carrier at the back for raincoats, etc. We had to make our own sandwiches before breakfast - a table in our common room had piles of bread and plates of sandwich 'stuff'. What a selection! Cheese, cheese, cheese, beetroot and one small dish of sardines! So we got wise. First up got the sardines.

The sandwiches made, you then had to rush out for a bike! There were twenty six bikes, but only half of them roadworthy! Faulty brakes, no lights, etc, so you dashed out to strap your sandwiches onto a decent bike!

Some Saturday nights we would cycle - twenty six of us - to a dance in Nuneaton, and we were lucky if two bikes had lights! So we would go in a long gaggle with a bike with a light in front, and a bike with a light at the back. Wouldn't dare do it now - and, of course, the roads were not lit in the blackout!

was in bed for a week, she never once came to my room. A young lady who lived in the village and worked with the horses brought me food. And yet the old farmer was so religious. After milking the cows, before we could have breakfast we had prayers, readings etc. Then breakfast - the same every single day - cold boiled FAT bacon and beetroot. No eggs allowed, as these

We didn't get travel vouchers like the forces did - well, you got two a year, so we had to pay our own fare home if we went for a weekend. I got the train at Tamworth, and it came from Birmingham! Always packed with soldiers, airmen, etc; so full that people were wedged in the corridors. Yet when the train stopped at Tamworth, the soldiers would shout "It's the Land Army, come on girls". Windows would open, and they would drag us in by the shoulders. The forces had a great respect for the Land girls, and would not have let us miss a train. Often we travelled home through the night - leaving for home after finishing work. One night, we had to change at Westby at 3.00 am, and had a long wait for the Leeds train. We went into the Y.M.C.A. for a cup of tea and the woman refused to serve us as we were not the forces. A soldier standing there asked how many of us there were. "Twenty six" we said. He then said to the woman "I want twenty six cups of tea, and you can't refuse to serve me!"

Working on the land was hard work, but I enjoyed every moment of it! Plenty of good laughs and fun in spite of the hard work.

We got no gratuity, of course, as the forces did! I did not even get any clothing coupons, so family chipped in for my wedding dress etc.
I came out just before the war ended, as I had a lot of sore throats! I went to the Doctor in the village, who said I needed my tonsils out. I could either go into Coventry Hospital or go home.

Frankly I thought the Doctor was potty as I'd had my tonsils out when I was small. I went home, saw my own Doctor, who said "Hospital straight away for tonsils out". It seemed that when I was small they had only been cut, and had grown again. I was then 24, and by the time I was OK, the war was about over. Thus ended my W.L.A. days.

Dorothy Newton
Skipsea, East Yorkshire

DOROTHY IN FULL UNIFORM

I have lots of funny things of L.A. days which could interest you.

Sheila Fishman (nee Trober) was one of those girls quite 'green' when it came to country life.

One foreman gave her a half filled bucket of corn, told her to go down the field to the hen pens and bring back all the eggs. Sheila did exactly that, pot ones and all. She had stacked the eggs all on top of the corn, thinking the farmer had put it in the bucket to prevent the eggs from breaking.

Sending Sheila down to a 'bottom field' with a cart full of manure, the farmer said "Don't forget to come at 12.00 for lunch". Sheila happily put out the piles of manure, and spread some before she went back to the farm at 12.00. "Where's the horse and cart?" asked the farmer. "Down the field" replied Sheila, who hadn't thought to bring them up with her, and left the poor animal standing there hitched up to the cart. Poor Sheila never went back to the farm, at the farmer's request.

Dorothy Gordon (nee Organ) was seventeen and a half years old when she joined us. She always said that when she got married, she would love to have twins. Having said this to one farmer, he said he could help her achieve this by letting her have double yolked eggs each day to take back to the hostel for breakfast. Poor Dorothy had eaten several of these before she found out they didn't work that way.

One of our girls, Joyce Pickles (we used to kid folk she was the late Wilfred Pickles' niece) had a dreadful high pitched squeaky singing voice. Joyce and I were sent to a farm where one of the farm hands, Simon, who was nearer 80 than 70 years, couldn't stand Joyce singing and kept telling me this, also asking me to "shut her up".

Simon and I were in the shippon milking one afternoon. Simon was milking a cow opposite the door when in walked Joyce singing. He turned the cow's teat up towards Joyce and no-one was more surprised than him when he scored a "bulls eye" in Joyce's face. She never sang in his presence again, much to his delight.

A dear friend, Lea Childs, who I'm sad to say died when only 51 years old, came to work with me on her first day in the W.L.A. My friend Gwen Bull was already working with me, and we had been asked to bring another girl to help with the hoeing.

Working in the field near to the farm we could hear pigs squealing. I knew the farmer was having one killed for his own use, so when she asked "Why all the noise?" I told her of the 'killing' and said probably the other pigs sensed what was to happen. "How will the pigs be killed?" asked Lea. "Oh", I said in fun "the butcher and farmer tie a wire around its neck and pull each end 'til it chokes". Lea went mad with threats to report them to the RSPCA until I told her the truth. I couldn't believe she'd fall for that.

Brenda Hughes and myself were sent to one farm, and as the farmer relayed his orders to us, Brenda and I were so fascinated by the wobbling of his only two teeth, we forgot half of what was said and had to go back and ask again, much to our embarrassment.

We found the smaller farms more generous. The big farms would only give you a drink when threshing, etc. We always had a good 'tuck in' at smaller farms.

When hay harvesting in my first year, four of us went to one farm, and the farmer took us all into a huge field and showed us how to cock the hay. He said "I'll leave you to it now, girls, and if you get thirsty there are flagons of cider dotted around the field - help yourselves". It was a scorcher of a day, and needless to say we quite often got a thirst on. We were all very happy working, singing and laughing. What the farmer didn't tell us was that the cider was a strong home brew. No wonder we were all 'happy'. He was a real sport, and laughed his cap off at us.

I was the prankster at the hostel and one or two of the jokes I played may interest you and make you smile.

The favourite with the girls is when I 'stuffed' my uniform and made a head out of a mango, and put my rear cycle lamp on it

to throw a ghostly red glow.

I had scared the head girl with it when I put it onto her bed and took out the bulb from her shade. She had a real fright when she saw it and went yelling down the corridor. I sat the 'body' in a chair in the middle of the corridor hoping to scare some of the girls as they either passed, or came down the corridor.

My dear friend Marjorie Frankish, coming up the back stairway, swinging her dance shoes, saw this girl out in the corridor, said "Hiya, kid", slapped her back and her head rolled off. Poor Marjorie fainted with shock and I flung the 'body' into my room before shouting for help. Poor Marjorie, all she could say when coming round was "her head dropped off".

I found a way to walk over the bedrooms and went haunting one night with two more girls. General Lloyd, who had owned the hotel prior to it becoming one, had died in the first room I had slept in, and rumour had it he walked now and then; this wasn't true, but we made the girls believe it was that night. All were on top of the main stairway when we finished, and some were ready for going home. Our warden at the time was Mrs Owen, a great sport. She soon found out I was the culprit and set the girls on me. We often laughed about it.

Another time I painted tiny spots on the face of Nora Shoesmith, with lipstick. The following morning, one of the girls from another room popped in to see Nora whilst I was in the bathroom, and she dashed down for the warden who came up, saw Nora and took the girl's word that she must have measles.

Nora was sent to sick bay and the doctor 'phoned for. By then, it had gone too far for me to 'own up'. Nora was taken water to wash, and yes, you've guessed it, all the spots came off. Doctor was cross and so was the warden, Miss Davis. She would never have seen the funny side to that.

Barbara Helwell

My experience of farming was whilst serving as a Land Girl during the years 1943 to 1947.

After four weeks' training, I worked in a small village in the North of Yorkshire. It was during this time I had my first taste of learning to milk a cow by hand. On one occasion, I was knocked off my milking stool by the notorious "Kicker", which all the farm hands were afraid of, suffering a painful wrist after landing in the midst of a pile of cow pats, much to the amusement of the other cowmen in the byre. As all the herd were black and white, it was difficult to distinguish each one, so I decided to stick a label on the said cow's rump.

My next assignment was to harness one of the cart horses and attach the roller behind. I was given instructions as to which field was to be rolled. (There were four).

"Blossom" knew her way around and we spent a very pleasant morning plodding up and down the field. I felt very pleased when I had finished by lunchtime, and reported back to my employer, who said "Well done, luv" and that he would send me out again if all was well. My spirits fell, however, when he called me over and said "Ay, luv, you've rolled a field wi'nowt in it". I suffered for some weeks when the news spread around the village.

This particular farm was 1,000 acres, quite large by some standards. It was mainly laid to corn, grassland and root crops.

We featured in the local newspaper during Harvest time when all hands took part. I had worked like a Trojan all day, but when the photographs appeared with the article, I was the only person who seemed to be standing doing nothing - once again, more teasing.

I did, however, shine when a power cut meant that the whole dairy came to a standstill and the milking machines could not be used. All the men were called in to help with the hand-milking of forty cows. Here was where my milking training came in useful, the head cowman and myself being the only two people who had mastered the technique. We accomplished this task with the aid of paraffin lamps and finished at ten o'clock that night. I was the blue-eyed girl from that day on.

I recall when working on a farm near Hawes, North Yorkshire, being left in charge whilst my boss went to Oban on a cattle buying trip, taking his wife and children also.

It was the custom to take our milk in

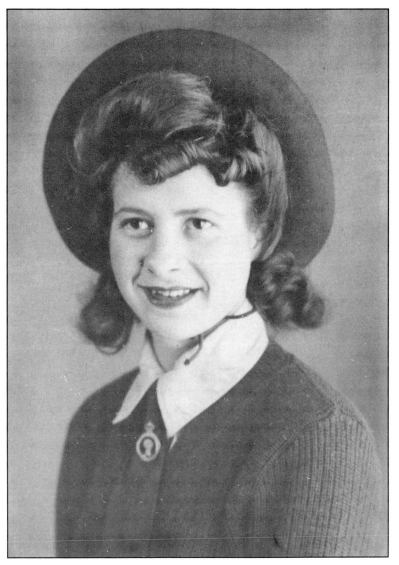

DOROTHY CHARLTON WHO SAYS THAT SHE WOULD NOT HAVE MISSED HER LAND GIRL DAYS FOR THE WORLD

15

churns and drop it off by the roadside where the Milk Marketing Board lorry collected it daily. This we took by horse and cart along a narrow lane; we collected the empty churns for the next day at the same time.

The horse I had taken was usually very quiet and placid, trotting along happily. However on my return journey this particular day something must have startled him as he suddenly put his ears up and started off at full gallop. He was rolling around and making the most awful noise, and the dog who had followed us joined in, barking excitedly to add to the confusion! I was frantically yelling "Whoa" at the top of my voice, as just ahead were two gate posts coming up fast, just wide enough to get through at walking pace. There was a crunching sound as the cart wheel caught one of the posts, bringing it to a sudden stop; the horse was on its knees and the cart sides broken. I landed on the horse's back very shaken and bruised, while the horse moaned and snorted, completely winded. I decided to unharness him and try to get him onto his feet, but he would not budge. After what seemed an age of pushing, pulling and pleading he suddenly got to his feet, shook himself and walked over to the trough for a drink. After checking the horse for injuries and finding all was well, I led him to the field to graze.

My bruises lasted for some time, but the one thing running through my mind as we galloped along the lane was, would my teeth be alright?

I had previously lost my two top front teeth in an accident and had two false teeth. Being a young girl, I was very conscious of them and never told anyone I had them. However, they survived the little pile-up. When my boss returned home I related the whole sorry tale, expecting a rollicking for breaking the cart, but he was more concerned that I was alright - what a relief! He could hardly believe our quiet cart horse had taken off. However, a few days later whilst muck spreading with the same horse, he took off again, with the farmer swearing and yelling after him, to no avail. Shortly after, the horse was sold.

One winter the weather was awful with rain every day flooding the yard. The midden heap ran alongside, surrounded by a narrow wall. On this particular day I decided to use the wall to walk on instead of splashing through the yard. Dressed to kill in my so'wester and long black raincoat, which reached my ankles (being five foot two and a half inches tall), I was carrying a bucket of eggs which I had just collected. Suddenly, the wind caught me unawares, I lost my balance and landed waist high in the midden. All I could do was laugh, as I was stuck fast. I managed to wriggle my feet out of my welly-boots and scrambled out. What a pong! I had a wash in the trough amidst howls of laughter from the boss and his wife. I had lost all the eggs, plus the bucket (It turned up in Spring!).

My weekly pay for working 6 am to dark was

the princely sum of twenty five shillings plus board and lodging. No wonder the farmers liked the Land Girls. When I went on leave, I was given a whole Wensleydale cheese, home churned butter, bacon from the pigs we kept, fresh eggs and a collie puppy in a cardboard box with holes. I travelled by train and when I arrived home my Mother said it was just like Christmas (everything was rationed at the same). The poor little puppy cried all night so my Father gave it to our milkman the next day who lived on a farm. I was very upset to lose it.

During the winter of 1947, heavy snow fell and all the roads were blocked. I recall a bus being buried in a snowdrift. The snow then froze and transport was at a standstill, apart from three pit ponies and traps which were used for delivering the milk. The milk was taken round the village in a churn with half-pint and pint measures. Customers brought their own jugs out to collect it.

We also sold potatoes, the supply in the shops having dried up. We had to dig ours out of "Potato Pies" built in the corner of a field, which were covered with straw and soil to keep the frost out. We sold these like hot cakes, rationing each person to half a stone to ensure that everyone had some. What a welcome we got, and a nice mug of tea in return.

Many different types became Land Army Girls. One in particular I remember came from the City of London and always covered her nose when mucking out the cows. She renamed the "belly band" on the horses a "stomach strap" because she thought it sounded too vulgar!

I had many more experiences during my farming days. Working on the land was very hard work, but also rewarding and healthy. I wouldn't have missed it for the world. My brothers and sisters enjoyed listening to my escapades as much as I enjoyed telling them. Yes, the W.L.A. days were enjoyable and ones that I often recall.

Dorothy Charlton,
E Gomeldon, Salisbury

Remembering a day at Queenbridge W.L.A. Hostel

Rudely awakened from slumber, certainly not by choice
"Come along girls, it's half past six", speaks the Warden's voice
Slowly the message penetrates, into life my limbs jerk
I realise it is morning, and I must prepare for work.

Grab the "sponge bag" and towel, make a dash for the loo
Then quickly to the washbasin before there begins a queue
Don overalls and milking slop, maybe tie scarf round the head
One more job before breakfast bell, and that is make the bed.

A 3 course breakfast awaits us, that's one thing we could boast
Porridge or cornflakes, bacon and egg, followed by marmalade on toast
The head girl reads out the rota; your farms she would allocate
Then it's pack your lunch, grab your bike, hope to be at work by eight.

The jobs you got would vary, maybe "general farm work" all day
Or depending on the season, threshing, corn harvest or hay
Happiness when farming could often depend on your boss
Some could be kind and caring, others wouldn't give a toss

Hoeing, cutting thistles, spreading "muck", pile after pile
Topping and tailing mangles, or "mucking out" pigs for a while
Maybe winter you'd work the potato clamp or be on a threshing machine
Where, should you be put on "chaff", you'd be a sight to be seen.

You'd sit down lunchtime, attack your lunch, mostly the same it would seem
Peanut butter, chocolate spread, and maybe last night's cheese dream
But if you were lucky, and had a good farm, they'd invite you to a taste their "fayre"
The big farms seldom, the smaller farms always, we found were willing to share.

When work ended, about 5.00 pm, back to the hostel you'd go
Thinking of things that made you laugh, or of moments full of woe.
You'd hope for a vacant bathroom, if none, you'd moan like hell
For then you'd have to hang about until after dinner bell.

You'd sit and enjoy a good dinner, even if you'd ate well all day
Yet "fair do's" we didn't get fatter, our figures remained the same way
At night each would do their own thing, maybe pictures or sometimes a dance
Some would stay in writing letters, some would be out for romance.

Some of us sat in the lounge, and laughed at our day on the farm
Or we'd play tricks on the girls, none of us meant any harm
Prompt at 9.30 the bell rang to say supper was on the table
Come and get your cocoa and fruit cake, enjoy a "cheese dream", if you're able

We'd have to "report in" 10.30; on that the warden was keen
If you didn't, she'd give you a lecture, asking you where you had been.
But we enjoyed the life, glad to help boys who'd been sent over the sea.
Leaving the land to such as us to "Dig for Victory"

Of the time we lived together, none of us could complain
And for years now we have proved it, by meeting again and again.

Barbara

18

Five years in the Women's Land Army

*E*ver since I'd reached 17, I had always begged my Dad to let me join one of the forces. It was late 1940 and I wanted to do my bit for my country. I took the countless forms home for him to sign but he was adamant, that was until the day I took home a form for the land army. Dad signed without any fuss at all. I was so thrilled and looked eagerly for the post from then on so as to know where to go to be kitted out. Before I knew it sixteen of us were sent to a house at Burnham-on-Crouch. We met the lady who was to look after us and were given a card to write home to our parents saying we had arrived safe and sound. We were then given our rooms and told to unpack.

We introduced ourselves to one another. I think we all found that it was our first time away from home, so we all had a common bond. On that first day we didn't have to work so we strolled around the town. As most of us were Londoners we couldn't get over how quiet it was, after all the bombing in London that we had left. It was absolute heaven! It was only a little town with just a few shops in the high street. One of the shops was a photographers. We were all looking in the window at the photos and decided that we should all have one done to send to our parents back home, so they could see our uniforms. We had no idea when we would see our parents again and this was a real adventure.

The following morning a lorry came to take us to the farm. Once there the foreman was waiting with us and he had a lot of hoes... 'Gels', says he, 'I want you to hoe this field of cabbages' he showed us these little tiny seedlings with all the big weeds round them. We all started off in rows, and hoped that we had left the right things standing - only time could tell us that! Sometime later the foreman took us back to show us our handywork... I've never seen a field that had so many bald patches!! I'm glad to say our work did get better as us old townies got used to country life. We did a lot of field clearing, hedging and ditching. The later I liked very much - I suppose because I was so big and strong. Some of the girls couldn't take the life and went home after the first few weeks.

Life was quiet until we began going to the dances which were put on for the soldiers who were billeted quite near to us. Now most girls from London way know how to dance as every town has its own dance hall or Palais de dance, so it becomes almost a way of life. So once we got on the dance floor with all our fancy steps, we had partners queueing to dance with us all evening. I'm afraid the local girls didn't like us one bit; looking back now I can't say that I blame them.

Some of the places we were sent to were really bad. At one farm we nearly had a riot. The farmer had two sets of horses ploughing up the field, we had big sacks tied around our middles to pick up the potatoes in before emptying them into the sack. We had had a lot of rain so the potatoes had so much mud clinging to them that it was very heavy going.

It had started to rain again but this farmer had kept us going. He kept cracking a whip all the time. The girls were exhausted and finally the last straw was when he knocked one of the girls down with a horse. We stopped work and one of us went to find a house with a phone. We rang the lady at the war agg. She said to hang on there until she could get someone down to see us. After about half an hour the lady arrived. She was utterly appalled by the conditions that we were working under. She told us to pack up and go back to the billet. She also told the farmer that he would never have Land Girls again. We all cheered like mad. She put the girl who had been injured into her car and took her to the nearest hospital. Fortunately for her it was only bruising - no broken bones. That was a really bad farm and we were glad we didn't have to go back there again.

It didn't take long for us girls to find boyfriends, but I'm afraid things now went from bad to worse with the local girls. One night it blew up into a big fight with everybody in it. The army lads were having a go at the local lads and the local girls were having a go at us! It did get quite out of hand and there were quite a few injuries. The following day, down came the lady from the war agg who was very, very angry. Two of the girls were sent home and the rest of us were split up and sent to different places. My little friend Daisy cried and said she didn't want to have to make a new friend but when the papers came we were the only two who were left together. We were sent to a place called Rockford not very far from Southend. This was a very big house standing in its own grounds and the lady who looked after us was very nice, but we hated it!

Because there were so many girls it was rotas for everything, including work. So, in the mornings you would go off in your groups to do whatever had to be done. By now we could do most things - hay making, hay stacking. Daisy and I had nearly died at Burnham taking down a stack that had fired, we had been very ill and apparently it was the fumes. From this day to the next I cannot stand the smell of whiskey because that is what the fumes smelt like. We used to go for long walks exploring in the lovely summer evenings.

One evening we walked further than we intended to and it looked as though we were going to be late in. As we had been on our best behaviour, we didn't want to be in the dog house. A car was coming along so we thumbed a lift as whoever was in the car would have to go past our billet. The man stopped and we asked him if we could have a lift as we were going to be late if we had to leg it back. We got talking on the way back and he asked us if we would like to be milkmaids on his farm - he neither lived on it or worked on it. His foreman had called him because the lads who did the milking had gone in the army. We said we would love to have a go but would have to get permission first form the war agg as we seemed to belong to them.

We asked the lady who was in charge of the house what she thought about it, and she said she would get in touch with the war agg. The lady came down to see us the following day and said it would be better if we tried it out first before committing ourselves to one job as we might not like it. That made sense. She gave us this address to go to, but when Daisy and I got there it wasn't the right farmer. We phoned our man up and we said we didn't know what had happened but we were on another farm. When we told him which one he did his nut.

It turned out that they were the two biggest land owners in the district and there was already a lot of bad feelings between them. I thought 'whoops, here we go again', when he phoned up the war agg. I don't know what went on, but down came the lady again saying, 'now I have two farmers fighting over you'. We said as we had given the first farmer our promise we thought it was only fair that he should have us. She agreed and phoned the second farmer saying he could have two more girls.

We were to go on a fortnight's trial before we moved in with the cowman and his wife in case we didn't like it. That fortnight nearly proved our undoing. The work we found really interesting. Time seemed to go so quickly even though you were up at the unearthly hour of 4.30 to start getting the cows in from the fields. The cowman's wife would bring over a cup of tea at about 7.30, then you worked on until the cows were finished being hand-milked and let out into the fields again. Then it was home to breakfast, and boy, did that taste good! You then mucked out, cleaned and washed out all the cow sheds. You took out the horses with a feed for the cows - depending on what time of the year it is or gathering the stuff for the silo for winter feeding, then you'd have a light lunch. We got a couple of hours to do what we liked before we got the cows in at 4 o'clock for the milking round once more. I didn't think at first that I was going to be able to carry on with it, my hands were blue and swollen up like balloons, but when I went to see the quack he said as soon as the muscles grew used to the strain of pulling on the teats day after day they would grow stronger - it was only a question of time.

Daisy and I both wanted to stay on even though we were both dog tired by the time we got back to the hostel. The end of the first week all the girls had gone home for a holiday weekend so there was only Daisy and I and the woman who ran the house. We asked her if we could have a later pass on the Saturday night as we would like to go to the dance down at the R.A.F. base at Stansted as we had not been out all week. She said we could. So off we went a happy as Larry! We had a smashing time at the dance and although several people wanted to take us home we said no.

We decided to take a short cut across the fields so that we could stay the last quarter of an hour before the dance ended, and we could be home for 12 o'clock. We came out of the dance and started to run home and horror of horrors we heard someone running behind us. We became very frightened as whoever it was was gaining on us. It was a couple of soldiers we had never seen before and really nasty pieces of work. In our day the fellows respected the fact that you were a virgin and we had never had any trouble before. But as I said, these two were really nasty. The fact that they were drunk didn't help either. One of them began to manhandle Daisy and I could see that we were not going to get anywhere even if we started fighting them. So I began to give them a tongue lashing and told them my dad would give them both a spell in the glass house if they didn't leave us alone. I made up some cock and bull story and it was so convincing that it seemed to be penetrating their thick skulls! The one that had grabbed me shouted to his mate to leave Daisy alone or this....(the a load of unrepeatable swear words)... bitches bloody father will have us in the nick. They started lumbering back the way they had come. Daisy and I ran and wept at the same time, only to find that when we had got to the house we had been locked out. Now the flood gates really did open up as we stepped back on the gravel path to call up to the lady's bedroom to come and let us in. We saw then as we thought, the lady, up in the attic. She was swinging a lantern so we yelled

at her to come down, when up popped her bedroom window. We knew we were the only ones who were supposed to be staying there over the weekend. In between our sobs we told her our story. We asked 'who is that on the top floor with a lantern?' At this she was very alarmed. She said we should all go upstairs and find out.

We all travelled upstairs to the top floor and looked in on all the rooms. Nothing could be found. Telling the story to the locals sometime late they said we had seen the ghost of one of the maids who had a boyfriend who was a sailor. When he was due home she would light the lantern for him to see his way clear to her. Apparently he had drowned and she had committed suicide because she couldn't live without him. So, we had now seen a ghost as well as almost being raped.

The lady made us cocoa and gave us each a couple of biscuits. She said she would wake us up in time to go to work. We didn't have to go quite so early, as the cowman's wife said she would give a hand until we arrived. We had about 4 hours sleep and were glad the following weekend when we moved in with the cowman and his wife. It made life that much easier.

We got used to the routine, and quicker at all the jobs. Soon we were able to start going out in the evenings. We went to this little pub in our village, the landlord used to be a London copper who had retired to the country with his wife. We really did have a lot of fun there. It got to the stage where Daisy and I would serve behind the bar just for fun. We had dart matches and parties. The baker who was next door would bake sausages and onions in his bread oven - they did taste good!! We had some really good nights, and it was there that I had my 21st birthday party. My mum and dad, and sisters came down and stayed until the Sunday. Everyone said it was a wow of a party and my mum was happy having seen for herself how happy I was. Although she got a bit of a shock the following week when a German plane was shot down just a short distance from our farm. She would have had kittens if she had known that I saw the pilot, just before he was shot down.

It happened like this.... We had just finished our lunch and Daisy said she wanted to write to her boyfriend before we went into town. So as it was a lovely day I decided to wait for her in the back garden. I was looking at a lovely rose when I heard the plane. I thought, 'My God, he's far too low'. When the plane came over the hedge the pilot was looking right at me. I shouted 'you're too low' and pointed upwards. I had just got indoors and said to Charlie the cowman, 'another four foot and he'd have hit the hedge' It was then that we heard a terrific bang. I didn't know what had happened until my mother phoned up and said she had heard on the radio about this German plane being shot down. I said that that must have been the bang that we heard. But that incident, coupled with a few other things that happened to me before I went into the land army has now made me a fatalist. That pilot could have shot

me down where I stood! There was a report in the local paper that at the pilot's funeral, there was a woman who came in black and never spoke to anyone. I know a lot of my friends thought it was me. But I have no idea who it was and although I had cause to be thankful to this unknown pilot, it was certainly not me at his funeral.

Our life at this time was hard work and a delightful night life, so we were very happy. At one of the parties at the pub we had a smashing time. It was Bill the publicans birthday. Daisy wasn't there as it had been a long weekend and she had gone home. When it was time to go home, one of the fellows at the pub who shall remain nameless said he would take me home. I said 'no thanks'.. He had made plenty of passes at me before, but there was something about him that I didn't like. Bill seeing all of this going on turned to his wife and said that he would see me to the turnstile. So he told me to hang on a while and he would take me. I was very grateful. We walked across the three fields, we were talking and laughing about the party and saying what a good time we had had. We came to the stile and I hopped over and said 'I'm okay now Bill, thanks for seeing me home.' 'Goodnight, see you tomorrow.' I went home to bed and I didn't need any rocking.

I got up with the lark although I'd only had three hours sleep, I didn't worry. Daisy got back from her leave in time for her afternoon milking and we chatted about her leave and the party while we worked. When we had finished we washed and changed, had dinner and were off down to the pub. When we opened the door there was an uproar. In one voice they all yelled 'what did you do to Bill last night'. I said 'nothing', mystified, when Eddie said 'stop teasing her'. I said 'where is Bill' and she said 'I'm afraid he's in bed love, Doc's orders.' I was horrified and wanted to know what had happened. She said that when Bill wasn't back after half an hour she was worried and a couple of the people who had been helping to clear up said they would take a look to make sure he hadn't fallen down in a ditch. The found him slumped down to the ground not far from the stile. They managed to get him back home when Eddie, seeing the look of him sent for the doctor, who said he had had a slight heart attack and had to stay in bed for a week.

Daisy and I went up to see him. He said he felt okay and didn't know what all the fuss was about. We said 'the doc said that you have to stay there so that's what you will do'. It wasn't long after this that I suffered an awful pain in my left ear. I was home for my Summer holiday at the time, and I went to see the doc who sent me to see a specialist at the London hospital. He said I had to go in as it was a mastoid I had, and had to have an operation. Because of the bombing in London, all the hospitals had annexes outside London. So off I went the following day when I had informed the war agg. and my boss where I would be. When I came too after the op there was a young doctor sitting by my bed. My first thought was who the hell had hit me in the jaw. It was so painful that I didn't think about my head!! I said as much to the doctor, and he told me not to worry as he would get something for the pain. Anyway, being as tough as old boots I survived, but of course, when the bandages came off I looked a right mess. I only had half a head of hair!! That was a small price to pay for a life.

A woman came to see me from the war agg. and said that when I was well enough I was going to a convalescent home run by the Red Cross for service women. It was a place called Ondal, nr Peterborough. Came the day that I arrived there it was a beautiful mansion some kind lord had sent to the Red Cross for the duration. It was set in a beautiful garden and someone told me it had an all glass ballroom - but I didn't get to see it.

The lady in charge had a Joyce Grenfell voice and was very sweet. I soon felt on top of the world in such a beautiful setting, and on being well enough to go outside the house, a few of us girls decided to go and look around the village. It was there that I met my first Yanks. They were fresh over from the States and had been briefed as to what girls were short of in Britain. We were bombarded with silk stockings, Max Factor make up, chocolate bars and chewing gum. We thought Xmas had come all over again. To say we girls were overcome with all this generosity would be an understatement, but as the lads were going on to we knew not where, I thought it would be a nice idea to write to some of their mothers telling them what nice lads they had, and how we appreciated the gifts that they had brought us. That is how I had my first letter printed in an American newspaper. One of the mothers that I had written to thought it would be nice to let all the other mothers know of my letter. Perhaps it helped them adjust to the fact that their sons and maybe their husbands were far away.

After I had finished my convalescence, I had to go back to see the specialist who had done my mastoid operation. He said that I would no longer be able to go back to milking as the cows have a habit of flicking their tails around your ears and he said it was too much of a risk. So once again I was moving on in the Land Army. Daisy was staying on at the farm as her boyfriend was due home soon, and they hoped to get wed, so she didn't think her stay in the Land Army would be for that much longer.

I ended up in a place called Nazeing which is about six miles from Epping Forest. They had dug up the golf course and planted it with potatoes, wheat and barley and made the club house in to a small hostel for us with bunk beds all in the one room. I think there were sixteen girls in all, plus the housekeeper. There were two baths and a row of six sinks. The girls were all very nice and I found myself to be the longest serving member of the Land Army.

The crops on the common were mostly done with machines, apart from the potato picking, which we did. We travelled to other places in lorries and some of the girls went on bikes. I was doing mostly land-clearing, hedging and ditching, which I enjoyed, although I must say we led our foreman Bert one hell of a dance. At the time I was going with an Army dispatch rider and if he was ever anywhere near us he would give us a toot, and off I'd go for a spin around the country lanes, the other girls covering up for me with the foreman saying I had been taken short.

I remember on one of these trips going through a little village, when Bert shouted 'quick, put your scarf over the number plate. It's my commanding officer'. I yanked the scarf off my head and held it behind me. We turned the first corner we came to and doubled back to where I was working. When we stopped, Burt said that he hoped the officer hadn't seen his number plate because if he had, he would be in the glass house. Apparently, it was quite against all army rules to give lifts to any civilians. I never saw him again after that day, so I couldn't say what happened to him.

On another farm we worked on, soldiers were camping and there were quite a few rows between the farmer and the camp commandant. Apparently the farmer kept losing a lot of little pigs and chickens. He kept going to the commandant saying that his men were thieving them. The commandant would have none of this. He would retaliate by saying us Land Girls kept his men's mind off what they were supposed to be doing. One day one of the soldiers asked us if we would like to go to supper with them. They told us where it was to be held, and we borrowed enough bikes to get us there. I must say they did us proud. I'm afraid to say we were never in any doubt where the farmer's pigs and chickens went.

Up at the Golf House we had many dinners of partridge eggs which we found up on the common. The only fly in the ointment we could see was our supervisor. There was definitely something odd about her. The food was horrible, sugar was hardly ever seen, although she had the ration books, so we girls were always hungry. Another girl and I went to see her about the appalling food. At this she got very angry. That same evening a fried of mine had gone into Wapping to see her boyfriend, to whom she was engaged. She had said that she might be a little late, so I was to make all the necessary arrangements. She meant that I was to go into the office, get the key and unlock the door for the one coming in late, lock the door and then put the key back in its place. It was only because it was a special occasion, and our housemother was in a bad mood with us that she wouldn't give her a special pass. It was about 11 o'clock when my friend got back. She did the necessary, had her wash and then went straight to bed.

Suddenly, the lights went on and in stormed our house mother. 'How did you get in?' she said. My friend replied through the door, where upon the poor woman went berserk and her last words were that we could all get up and make our own breakfasts. The girls were all up in arms at this

and asked me what they should do. I said if she didn't call us we should all stay where we were and I would get up and telephone the war agg. In the morning the housemother was all dressed up to go out. As soon as she was gone I went into the office and telephoned the war agg. When I told them what had happened they said to sit tight and they would get someone down to sort it all out. At 11 o'clock out came a woman in a car, they had brought bread and cheese with them. By this time were all starving hungry. They told us to eat first and then we would all have a talk. When we had finished eating we told of our grievances, and the fact that we were all being cheated out of our rations. I don't think that they believed this. At this moment one of the girls said 'look who's home' and walking along the main road was the housemother.

The women took her into the office after packing us girls off saying they would get our lunch for us. When we arrived back for lunch our former housekeeper was packing her things and then a taxi came and took her away. They said that they had found out why we were so short of food, they showed us a cupboard which was full of our rations. There was about 1cwt of sugar alone. God knows what the woman had been thinking of. We were all told that there was someone coming in to look after us. When she came she was not that much better than the one that had just left. We wondered where they dug them up from! Anyway, she didn't stay long, she had to go back home to look after ailing parents.

Then we had Greta and her two children, a small boy and girl who all us girls absolutely adored. Greta was a Dutch girl who had married an officer who was on the submarines and had gone down with the sub, I found out a lot later. Greta was a fine cook, very tough yet very fair with all her dealings with us girls and we were all very happy at last. The children were a delight to us all. Greta let us have a dance about once a month to which we invited some boys from some of the camps nearby. We had English and Polish airmen, army personnel, and once we had a Canadian and some Yanks. All in all we were having some fun but still working very hard.

It was about this time we had started playing with the Ouija board. Who had though of it I can't remember, although no-one believed in it. To us girls it was quite a game. we all took turns to ask it silly questions and got just as silly answers. As I said, we all thought it was just a joke until the night Nancy asked it where her brother was because he was missing. The glass just flew back and forth to the letters that spelt D.E.A.D. Nancy screamed and we were all very alarmed and hoped it wasn't true. As it turned out some weeks later, it was true. We never ever played with it again.

One night we were all in bed when we heard the phone ring. Greta answered it and we wondered who the bad news would be for at this time of night. Greta came in an said that it was the Police and the army needing our help. There was a German parachutist up on the common

somewhere and they wanted us girls to help the troops find him as we knew the common better than anyone else at that time. We had all got dressed and put on our wellies by the time the troops arrived. We were all given a section, a lamp and away went. We had all been potato picking that day and it was very difficult going as the last of the potatoes were still in the sacks and as it was a dark night it was hard to see them. I think that I mentioned before that Nazeing Common rolled up and down with little copses dotted about here and there. I should think it was a marvellous golf course before the war. We searched our section and went back and reported that we couldn't find anything.

Greta had got cocoa ready as we trudged back, party by party. When a whistle blew we knew he had been caught. In actual fact he hadn't been up on the common, he had dropped at the back of us and was caught by the people searching that bit. I·was about 4.30 am when we crawled into bed. It seemed we had only just got there when it was time to get up again. Life went on and as I've said before, some weekends, if we could afford the fare we would go home.

This week had been home and had had a very nice weekend. The friend I travelled with went further on than I, and we arranged to meet at Epping to walk the six miles back to Nazeing as the buses back finished so early. I got off my bus and waited for my friend and realised by now that she wasn't coming back that evening. So I thought, well old girl, you will have to do it on your own. When you are young a six mile hike seems nothing to you, especially when you are chatting about the things girls always chat about. You talked about all the fellows that you had met over the weekend, how your folks were and how they had coped with the doodle bugs, rockets, land mines and all the other horrible things that Hitler had thrown at us. We were very proud of our folks at home, they really had to put up with a lot.

Apart from a bit of strafing from the odd Jerry aircraft that had got lost or isolated incidents we suffered nothing at all in the country. But back to my walk. It was a very lonely road with a small farm here and there, a house and just a lot of darkness. I started walking and nothing sounded lonelier than my footsteps. I walked on and on and then horror of horrors I heard footsteps behind me; to say I was frightened would have been the understatement of the year. The more I hurried, the footsteps seemed to hurry too. By now I was in such a sweat that I couldn't have run even if I'd tried as my legs had turned to jelly. I gave myself a good mental shake and said that it was no good, you've got to turn around and face your assailant, you can't go on as you are. Making my legs obey me I turned around shouting as I did, 'look I'm not frightened, only to be stopped when I saw who was following me... one big cow... I was so relieved, cows I could deal with,. I put her into the first gate I came to and hoped the farmer would find her in time for milking the next morning. Everyone in the hostel had a good laugh at this episode.

My friend's mother had phoned the hostel to say that my friend had gone down with flu. We made many friends from our social nights and because we were all friends as opposed to being pairs they all knew that they were welcome to come and have a game of cards or darts whenever they could get time off in the evenings if they had transport. Most of our troops could only ever get over on our social evenings, when they were provided with transport by their officers. The Yanks seemed to have no such problems. There was a short period when we saw a lot of them. They were such a good bunch of fellows.

I well remember one guy who always called me 'Happy bottom'. I couldn't think why, and I blushed like hell when he told me. My Christian name is Gladys and if you split that in two in turns out to be Glad-ass, same sound, different spelling. I can remember getting a letter form this guy's sister saying she was writing for his mother who could not write in English as she was Italian. But the mama was worried about her son, as she'd asked him if there was anything he had wanted, and always the same answer, 'no, nothing mamma', would I please write and tell them if there was anything he was going short of. I wrote back and told them that their son was happy and had everything he needed except his family. Apart from some Yanks that I had met earlier, these were the only Yanks I had ever met and talked to. They were really charming guys.

I think the one thing that stands out in my mind

at this time was the fear that they all seemed to be suffering when they knew they were going into battle, it was almost a sense of doom. I had a very strange letter from one boy, and then no more from him, but I had one from his sister, desperate for news. I had none to give. I never knew what happened to him, although we did hear that an awful lot of first squad didn't make it. As I had written in my letter to his sister's parents, they could only wait and pray.

At about this time they were beginning to bring German prisoners of war to work on the common in small batches. I well remember one incident that could well have been nasty. Us girls were going hay pitching and were walking along the path with our hay forks when along the path came one tommy with a gun and eight prisoners. As they went past, one huge fellow spat at us girls. Nancy, our friend, who had lost her brother, went quite mad and flew at this guy with her pitch fork, screaming at him. I think she would have killed him with her bare hands let alone the pitch fork. But his little brave Tommy shouted 'stop or I'll shoot'. We pulled Nancy away from this very frightened Nazi, I bet he never spat at another English woman as long as he lived.

Soon after his there was talk about closing up the golf house. A lot of my time had been taken up at threshing time, going around with a team of four girls to all the farms with a threshing machine. I liked the job but it was very dirty, especially if you were on the chaff and caving. We all took turns at everything. If you were on

the stack, pitching up, you had all things like baby mice and rats dropping in your shirt front or a mouse running up your trouser leg! If you were on top of the machine, cutting string and feeding the machine, you took a chance with taking your finger off, or a lump out of it. And if you were taking the sacks off the back and tying them, remembering they weighed 100 cwt each, you stood a good chance of straining your back if you didn't get the lift right. So every job presented a hazard of some sort. One consolation, you were allowed in the bathroom to wash and change before anyone else, as I said, after a day of thre shing you looked and felt as though you'd been in a coal hole.

One day I was sent to a nursery which grew tomatoes and cucumbers. It was coming to the end of the season but I liked the work and asked the boss if he could fix it for me to work permanently there. He did and I went to a hostel quite near. It was totally different to the Golf House - even the girls seemed different. It was there when I discovered the very first bad case of head lice. I think there were about five girls in all. There was a great to do about two girls who were sleeping together. I didn't really understand what all the fuss was abut. Anyway, one of the girl's parents came and took her away. I don't think I realised it until years later, but these girls must have been the very fist lesbians I ever saw.

Greta had now gone with the children to stay with her husband's family, until she could get to South Africa where she was going to live with her brother. I missed seeing the children, and our talks, and I definitely didn't like this new hostel one little bit. Two of the girls in the Nursery were in private digs and one of them, Tilly, said she would ask her landlady if I could stay there. It was all arranged with the war agg. and once more I was in private digs. This suited me fine as I'd met the man who was to become my husband. Also, when one was in private digs one was not restricted to having a late pass. I stayed there for just over a year as my boyfriend had been sent to India. When he got back I left the Land Army and got married on the 17th August, 1946.

Gladys Wescott

I was a shop assistant from Hull and volunteered for the W.L.A. at the age of 17 years 9 months.

I was sent to Malton in Yorkshire and arrived on the doorstep of Yates & Sons, farm machinery suppliers, on an icy February morning, shivering in thin town clothing, my uniform having gone astray in transit. My job was to be hired out with a threshing team which consisted of the machine, steam engine, a driver, a fireman and two land girls. We were given 'War Agriculture' bicycles and instructed to follow the team within a twelve mile radius of our billet in Westow village.

My only experience of the country was riding through it as a keen cyclist, but I loved being out of doors; growing things in city gardens was a delight, so I soon got tuned in to the country life, though it seemed hard at first.

My workmate was to be a girl from Leeds, aged 21, also a beginner. The first problem was teaching her to ride the heavy bike - she had never ridden before and was nervous. After a few tumbles and giggles she got the hang of it and we were ready to start the first four miles.

The noise, dust and back-breaking 'chaff carrying' seemed a bit of a nightmare to me, but after a while we got used to it and I decided that if I was stuck with a winter season of tramp threshing, I had better get more efficient so that

I could get away from the dreaded chaff carrying. After a short course and a test, I got a proficiency badge and was able to work among straw stacking, building up the corners as good as a man, heaving bales about and threading the baler with wire. I could perch on top of the machine, feeding the roller drum with sheaves of corn, or band cutting for the feeder. We did this job daily until Easter and after a week's holiday back in Hull, we were sent to do field work at a farm in North Grimston, and the two of us stayed there until after harvest when the threshing was once again loaned out for the Winter season.

We were a good working partnership, Edna and I, and soon learned to put up with each other's idiosyncrasies. She was not used to going out at night too much, so sometimes I joined forces with other land girls in Malton and enjoyed dancing at the Milton Rooms and the village venues. I remember the wonderful music from the band of the Cold Stream Guards who would play delightful military two steps and rousing quick steps every Saturday night. Malton became the Guards Headquarters, so there were often interesting events going on.

Our living accommodation in Westow was not a happy arrangement, so the District Commissioner, Lady Howard Vyse, helped us to find more suitable lodgings and soon we were delivered by her car to Langton to stay with Mr and Mrs Bradley in a cottage. She looked after us very well and became our second Mum. I have nothing but praise for her. Isaac, her husband,

IRIS FAULKNER

was a woodsman and gamekeeper for the Langton estate and he helped us a lot, a true countryman like his father before him. The name

Isaac Bradley is still gathering moss on the village memorial stone.

We cycled many miles to work. I used to envy the land girls who passed in lorries, driven from their hostel to the farms. They always looked happy and sang in unison wherever they went. I missed the comradeship they obviously found in groups, but the family life in the cottage had its own rewards, and as we sat on the pricked hearth rug by the log fire, Isaac would tell yarns about his youth on the farms and lots of folk-lore. I can still smell the paraffin lamp and the home-made beeswax, the stored apples in boxes and the bacon hung from the ceiling; the goose grease he used on his chest for his cough, the dubbin from our boots as they dried off near the fire and the dung which lingered on our overalls and breeches.

Our days in the fields were mostly enjoyable, though hard work and tedious in the rain. I enjoyed hay making, tossing the loads into the carts and riding the horses home. No-one told us how to ride, or even fix a harness; they presumed we knew all these things once we wore a uniform of the W.L.A. My first experience was memorable. The harness was not fixed properly and off I slid, under the belly of the horse, and was dragged along the rough lane, hanging on like grim death. I had to be helped up and pinned up! As the foreman said "My rear end was a sight for sore eyes!" I was a long time living that down.

No-one ever told us about wearing a mask to mix the pink chemical powder into the corn until I had been doing the job for eight hours and had a breathing problem and great discomfort. We were supposed to know about these things! However, we survived and stayed happy most of the time.

I enjoyed scything thistles, standing in a row of three or four workers, working across the pastures. Being left handed brought problems. I developed a powerful swing and a good rhythm, but my left handed action caused the unfortunate worker beside me to jump about to avoid losing a foot, as I swung the scythe in the opposite direction to everyone else. I was ridiculed as a 'cack-handed townie' and sent to the back. After that I worked twice as hard to prove myself!

I loved standing at the edge of the field with the long curved blade in the air as I sharpened it with a flint stone and a bit of spit, as taught by the 'thirdie lad', a kindly but slow-witted youth whom I nicknamed 'Fondie' after a book of that name. I wish I could find that wonderful book gain. What marvellous characters I met on the Wolds. The dialect was a delight to me and often I scribbled it in my diary.

Moving on to Driffield, Bainton and Mrs Barratt, I joined another threshing team. This time the old steam engine was replaced with a tractor and we lost the soot and smoke and inconvenience, but also we lost an old friend who had kept us warm on frosty mornings and hissed and sang to us as no other engine could.

We were billeted in North Dalton in the cottage of the widowed Mrs Wilson. She looked after us well and instructed her son to keep an eye on us at night. He used to escort us to the village inn for a shandy and we would sit in the snug room with a wood fire, and wonderful hot bread cakes would be produced from the oven, dripping with butter.

We used to enjoy the village dances where, for six pence or a shilling, we could dance our legs off in land army brogue shoes, a match for the farm boots our partners often wore. I remember the lovely refreshments provided by village ladies. Even with food rationing, they still produced deep apple pies filled with cloves, and crusty home made bread with pork dripping (if someone had killed a pig that week). I remember getting ready for these outings, washing by candlelight, or oil lamp if we were lucky, with one jug of hot water each. I often arrived at a dance with threshing dust in my eye corners and ears. The dim light made ablutions difficult.

Once a week we were allowed a bath. This was usually a three inch tub in the garden shed. The warm water came from the buckets passed from the kitchen boiler, which were heated from the fire. I never felt deprived of conveniences then; we felt lucky to have the privacy of a garden shed, and to feel clean was great.

I remember working in the fields with Italian prisoners of war who were stationed at Eden Camp in Malton. They used to sing opera as they worked, and a lot of them fancied themselves as romeos, and wrote love letters on toilet paper in pencil which they threw at us from their lorries. We used to giggle, but back away, being half afraid of the situation and not wanting to be caught fraternising with the enemy. They were clever craftsmen and often gave farm workers slippers they had made from 'Massey Harris Band' that was used to bind the sheaves of corn. The wooden carvings they did were beautiful and made me feel sad. They should have been sat by their own fireside carving for their families. War time is such a waste of time for families, apart from all the horror that goes with it, but the character building and the comradeship is a bonus prize and something from which we should all learn and benefit.

The last six months of my service were spent on a dairy farm in Wheldrake, near York. I got used to milking cows and mucking out the fold yard. The first few days brought a few bruises from unwilling cows and the odd gallon of milk was spilt as I fought to gain authority.

I finally left the W.L.A. through ill health at the end of 1945, and I still have a soft spot in my heart for the Wolds and its people, and feel a better person for having known them.

Mrs T Newbould,
Hull, Humberside

LAND GIRLS AT WORK

I was in the Land Army in the county of Northamptonshire, a time of hard work, long hours and some good times with the girls in the hostel and the local lads.

We did not meet G.I.s but we did meet the German P.O.W.s who were also working on the land. At first, we held ourselves quite aloft from these men; after all, our fathers, brothers, uncles etc were fighting in the war and they were the enemy.

After a very short time, we were pleased if they were working near us. They were such a boon to calloused hands, aching backs and heads. Our crew would finish their work and then come and help us girls to finish our rows, whether it be hoeing, potato picking or whatever.

On one occasion, it was so cold we could not feel our hands and we were trying to get turnips from frozen ground. The call of nature occurred and I had to answer. As you know, we had to use bushes or trees - no finesse in the fields! Well I undid the buttons, but no way could I do them up again. My fingers were frozen. After a while, one of the P.O.W.s came to see if I was O.K. I explained, and with no more than a smile he did them up for me and helped me back to the frozen fields. They then managed to get a small fire going for us so we could at least defrost our hands.

We were picked up very often by their trucks and given lifts, where we might have had to walk. They even managed to ask us back to their camp one evening to repay our kindness. It was they who were kind to us girls. I know they were not glamorous like the Americans but I would say they were just as welcome a sight when we were working. Several of our girls married the German boys and were very happy. The older men sometimes were not so friendly, but that is to be understood; we were on the whole very young and out for a good time, and they were our prisoners of war.

Not forgetting the British soldiers either. We had some grand times with the Tommies from a local barracks. They were highlights when they came for the evening. After the drinking and dancing we were never fit for work the next day, and we often wondered how on earth they got back safely. Not one was sober by the end of the evening and, of course, the journey home was made in PITCH BLACK along country lanes in those days; we were in the heart of the countryside.

My very first proposal of marriage came from a very tipsy soldier outside the hostel. What a thrill in those far off days; he then had to drive the truck back to camp. I often wondered if he remembered the Land Girl he proposed to.

When I think back to the work we had to do and the food we were given, it's a wonder we managed to get through. A screw of tea and a screw of sugar each for our cuppa, beetroot sandwiches and no marg if you used it at breakfast. No wonder on Saturday evenings after being paid we would get the bus into Northampton for fish and chips. The treat of the week, then the bus home to the village, the pub 'til closing time, the village hop until 11.45, and hope someone might walk you home and take you into Bambury the next day for the pictures (and pay for you). We never had enough money to do everything we wanted to do.

Mrs Elaine Seal,

Waltham Cross, Herts

I joined the Land Army from an Oxford Street office in 1942. I fibbed about my age, and my Father signed the form, not really interested in the details.

I went from the Blitz in North London to the depths of Norfolk. I loved the work, but unfortunately my billet on the small farm was very sparse and the food dreadful, but I made the best of a bad job.

Opposite was an American Aerodrome. The G.Is were doing many raids over Germany, day and night. After one visit, I remember one of the G.Is mentioned that Glenn Miller was coming to play

at the Airfield for a celebration 250 Mission Party.

I had to be in by nine o'clock if I ever went out (which was very rarely). My only outings were to the farmer's daughter-in-law, who took in American laundry and sometimes I would flirt with one of her visitors!

Anyhow, I got to that party. The fair was there, and I went on 'Chair O Phones'. You start low on the ground and proceed to go upwards. I was wearing my Land Army uniform, so had the ride to yells of 'Ride 'em, cowboy'. Sadly, I only heard ten minutes of Glenn Miller.

One day in late summer, I was cutting hay for the cowsheds and had just cleared and mucked out when there was a dreadful crash from up above. A fighter plane and bomber on practise had collided and fell some three minutes away in the bean field. I ran to it with the farmer screaming after me 'Don't go thar, girl'. Sadly, deeply embedded in the earth was the spreadeagled body of a young man dressed in black leather. The name tag around his neck was glinting in the sun. I knelt and read 'Lt K Beales, aged 23 years'. I recited The Lords Prayer; as a Jewish girl it was the only prayer I could think of. Before long, the lane was full of men, ambulances and jeeps. On a visit to the American Cemetery at Cambridge I searched in vain for his name and grave, but one day I shall try again.

Mrs Sally Ashford

Norwich.

Lamb of December

Melancholy hid the sun through its grey veil weeping,
Across the rounded slopes came wailing north winds sweeping.
Into my face, relentless and bitterly tearing,
Striking to the heart, cruel, unheeding and uncaring.

Benumbed my feet over hoof pitted land were stumbling,
Frozen, aching fingers with swinging knapsack fumbling,
Fool! To leave your home! Bright warmth of the city, remember?
Why did you leave it all for this uncouth brute December?

Head bowed against the wind, my own folly scolding,
And, in my protesting hands, new steel-cold shears holding.
Nine hours yet before I stumbled back, my steps retracing,
Hours of stale bread and cheese cold tea, and winter' rough embracing.

Suddenly, shocking the wind to silence came bleating,
Helpless and bewildered, intermittently repeating.
In a sheltered hollow, with its weary ewe lying,
Proudly by, a lamb of spotless purity was crying.

C M D Upton 53729
Bucks

I was in the W.L.A. during the last War. The work was unremitting and very strenuous - so much so that the few men on the farm poured scorn on us for putting up with it. It was a far cry from the graciously bucolic posters all over London asking for recruits. In fact, though this may be of no interest literally, after about a year I had a physical/nervous collapse and had to convalesce for six months before being directed into a PR job with de Havilland Aircraft.

Having just left the RADA, I was pot-boiling with ENSA at Drury Lane, but was called up willy-nilly on the grounds that I was not actually on tour at the time.

My home is in St Albans and three of us were allotted to a nineteen acre field on the Verulam estate nearby, with the intention of converting it into a market garden for the supplying of the Enfield Rolling Mills canteen, also belonging to Lord Verulam - a rather ambiguous bachelor, who later tragically died by falling from the Aswan High Dam, then dry. Very few of us (we were later augmented to seven) in those innocent days guessed at the implications of so eligible a man of 39 still being a bachelor (whether justified or not I do not know) and there was great competition in self-beautifying and attention-seeking on the few occasions when he rather self consciously paid us a visit of inspection. One particular girl, built like a horse and with shapeless features of a doughy consistency (this is description, not cattiness) had

no misgivings, but a sublime faith that, once seen, she would be the chosen Cinderella. There was something uncanny about this certainty, which no experience could shake.

I cycled about six miles each way to work; we started at 7 am and worked 'til 6 pm (plus Saturday mornings) with only a short lunch break. We made our own lunch, in an old outhouse attached to the home farm, and I have not been able to look at a cauliflower cheese since. The field was not just virgin land, but intacta, and the first few weeks were spent by the three of us simply collecting and disposing in tasteful cairns the rocks, larger than a human skull, with which it was strewn. The ground was like iron that summer and the farm lent us a superannuated hand plough, together with an old mare to pull it. She knew her business and was set in her ways and any effort to vary them had to be backed up with the more familiar obscenities - her language. Once, taking the 180 degrees turn, my leg got under her feet and her hoof scraped down my calf, removing a few ounces of flesh - also removed both sock and uniform shoe and buried them. Pouring blood, I had to limp back to base and after first aid, borrowed some old boots until I could be issued with another pair. The hoeing and weeding of iron-hard earth was like convict work, but eventually that virgin land produced a crop of varied vegetables of a size and beauty only seen in advertisements - and in copious abundance. SOS messages were from time to time received from the Enfield Rolling Mills, imploring us to put a brake on our output as, rather like the sorcerer's apprentice, they were literally inundated with produce. In the end, we harnessed our Old Faithful to a farm cart and perambulated St Albans selling superlative vegetables to the bemused housewives, who usually had to queue for every lettuce leaf, for a few pence. This made a welcome rest and break and was probably illegal without a licence, but we were never hindered. What happened to the proceeds I never knew or have completely forgotten - presumably they belonged legally to the Earl, but I don't think he ever saw them and we certainly didn't.

This is not strictly or logically connected with the Land Army, but occurred when I was coasting gaily downhill on my return from the farm. I felt a small thud on my breastbone followed by incredibly painful burning sensations in my bosom. I stopped and peered down my shirt to see a wasp entrapped in my bra and stinging my breasts as fast as its sting would go. Efforts to scoop it out only redoubled the attack and panic set in, as I had heard that one could die from multiple wasp stings. Careless of appearances, I threw off my hat, dragged up my jersey and flung it from me onto the grass verge, followed by my shirt. Still the wasp was inaccessible, so that finally (and thirty years before toplessness was countenanced and in spite of the presence of a sedate, elderly couple walking on the other side of the lane) I added my bra to the discard pile. I vaguely heard the man murmur something about "best ignore .... unfortunates". I realised that inside the high wall by the side of the lane was the district lunatic asylum (as we bluntly called them in those days). How he thought an inmate had come by Land

Army uniform, I didn't ask myself. I rode several miles home after putting my shirt back on, in such pain I could barely endure it. There were certainly a dozen stings, but they were impossible to count as the burning mass had coalesced. The pain lasted two days. If ever brassière should have been spelt brazier, it was then.

A less painful occurrence was that of the cider. I sometimes took a plain bottle of decanted cider in my bike basket to slake thirst during the day. This one early summer morning, I was cycling along a street in St Albans on my way to Gorhambury (the Verulam estate). There were small terraced houses on either side with the minimum of front garden. Suddenly, in the dawn hush, there was a sizeable explosion as the cork of my bottle flew upwards and rapped sharply on an upstairs window, the contents of the bottle effervescing up and flowing onto the road. As I saw the bedroom curtains being drawn, I thought it best to know nothing but, glancing over my shoulder, I glimpsed a buxom woman at the bedroom window and a man in pyjamas examining the front patch. Everyone was on the qui vive as we had several bombs and a land mine in the vicinity. I heard the word "shrapnel" but I could not tell if this was his diagnosis or whether he was re- assuring her that it could not have been.

At the home farm, on the days we did not brew a copper full of cauliflower cheese, I was in the habit of taking my thermos and sandwiches into a part of the cattle shed and climbing a three rung ladder into a huge pile of chaff or bran, which was very comforting to racked limbs. One day, while I was eating a sandwich, I heard a strange sound, between a sigh and a grunt, at my right elbow, and was immediately in a veritable snowstorm of chaff, which got in my eyes and settled thickly over my drink and sandwiches. This was disconcerting enough, but when the sandstorm settled a bit I saw, and still feel the shock, a few inches from my right arm, the solid brow of an enormous bull, about three feet in width, not counting the wicked looking horns, framed in a square hole in what looked, to my stricken eye, like matchboard. I had, and still have, a horror of animal heads (the mounted dead ones) and a live one, belonging to what I knew was a very powerful and temperamental bull, nearly paralysed me. He was regarding me quite peaceably with a puzzled "What's fallen into my lunch?" expression, but I rolled off my perch in reflex time (never mind the ladder) shaking, as they say, like an aspen leaf, and with no edible lunch.

I think it is in 'She Stoops to Conquer' that there is a celebrated story of the Grouse in the Gunroom, which is constantly referred to with uncontrollable laughter, but never related. So it is with my own story of 'The Goat at Gorhambury'. However, I will try to relate it now. There was a hoary billy goat attached to a chain on an iron stake in the middle of the farm yard. For some reason, he took an unreasoned dislike to me and used to butt towards me whenever I passed, at the limit of his chain, and dart hate at me from those otherwise vacant yellow eyes. I never saw him aggressive towards anyone else. One day, I passed on my own on the way to the loo, which consisted of a long (near to thirty feet) stone flagged passage. He made his usual hostile passes but I safely reached the sanctuary of the loo and thankfully shot the rather fragile looking bolt behind me. I could hear that his agitation was augmenting outside when, suddenly, with a noise like a travelling ironmongers, there was a ram (pun not intended) at the door. I think he had uprooted the stake but my eyes never focused subsequently enough to see. The bolt held, but after a run back each time, he renewed the assault. Finally, to my horror, the bolt and fitting skittered along the floor to my feet, followed by the maddened beast, horns low. Luckily, he made contact only with the porcelain pedestal, sending splinters in all directions. He made at least six of these runs, each time retiring deliberately to the open door to get a good run in.

The next thing I remember about myself was that I was standing on the pan (somewhat encumbered by the Land Army corduroys draped round my ankles) armed with the only available weapon of defence, the lavatory brush, and belabouring the granite forehead of the animal, like Horatius keeping the bridge in the brave days of old. Luckily for me, he charged each time with head down and succeeded only in sending more china splinters flying, but it became a battle of attrition. One cannot spend a whole afternoon standing on a lavatory seat doing battle with the brush and improperly dressed. I don't know how long it was - perhaps not as long as I thought - before the

39

farmer's wife arrived to claim him (luckily not the farmer, as I was very proper in those days) and collected him by the collar, laughing heartily (and heartlessly) at me while assuring me that he wouldn't hurt a fly. This may have been strictly true, but he had given such a long and convincing impersonation of an animal hell-bent on hurting me, as to convince me completely. When I finally tottered back to the work force, I was reproved for taking so long over my ablutions.

Margaret Wilkins

Remembering my memorable war years back in England, I was born on 9 August 1927, so I was a very young lady when war broke out. I was evacuated from Gravesend, Kent on 9 March 1939 to Wymondham, Norfolk, which were very miserable years for me except for a couple of years' stability with an elderly couple. In the later years I went from pillar to post. I was from a poor family, one of seven children, and survived a lot of rejection and insecurity.

At fourteen I was working at a brush factory - 8 am until 5 pm for the wage of 11s 2d, and at the age of fifteen added to that the job of part-time usherette at the local movie house.

Even though I was under age at sixteen I joined the Land Army, and spent some of my better days - hard work, but also exciting. I was stationed at Sea Palling, and did some of the most stupid but funny things. One day I drove the tractor into a pond, and ploughed up three rows of sugar beet while leading the horse, not watching where I was going because I had on my brown brogues instead of wearing the boots we were issued with. I was scared to death the horse would tread on me. Every so often, unannounced, an official would check up on us to see that we were doing our job properly.

There were only two of us at a lonely coastal farm, and many battles were fought there. We would climb a haystack to watch the British and German fighters. The American bombers would pass over on their way to targets and on the way back, flying low over the Channel. German fighters would mix in with them, and if my memory is correct they would not be picked up by radio. An American bomber crashed over the hills into the water. The hills were mined, and we went over with the farmer and rescued a member of the crew from the water. I had often wondered what happened to him. We called the Red Cross, and the Americans picked him up later. The aircraft lay there with the gunner that had been killed over Germany. That bothered us - we would go up and look at it, feeling sad as he looked to be young - around nineteen. The man we rescued took our names and I always wondered what happened to him because he must remember the girls who swam out to help him in.

I married a G.I. from the 8th Airforce in 1945. I went to visit the old base at Wymondham museum, and found a picture of me in uniform on the wall. I had been at a dance. At the time I worked for the American Red Cross, a van picked us up and we would hand out the coffee and doughnuts.

I have wonderful memories of those exciting war years. Fancy, we were grown up in those days at seventeen and a half. What glamorous, glorious, fun-filled days - but we worked very hard too.

Elizabeth O'Donnell,
New York, U.S.A.

I was seventeen and three quarters when I joined the W.L.A., posted to a farm on the Yorkshire Wolds. One of my first jobs was filling in bomb holes left by enemy aircraft. Wold land is very chalky, and it was hard work. I very soon had blisters on my hands. Another job I had was making up wicks (couch grass) - it was dried out, raked up into heaps and then burned.

I didn't stay very long at that farm. Mrs Blakestone, a very nice lady who lived in a big house in Driffield, did all the organising of the farms we worked on and organised meetings and rallies. Sometimes on Saturdays we would have to don our best gear; strong brown shoes, three-quarter length socks, breeches, and three-quarter length brown coats and wide brimmed hats.

I remember working on a 900 acre farm at Cottain near Driffield. It was a 24 horse farm, but when I went there were about 12 horses and 3 tractors. Some of our fields were two miles from the farm - "Low Balm" it was called. When we worked down these, we had to have a pack-up lunch. It was mostly cold tea in a bottle for a drink. I used to love it down there, working with the horses, harrowing or ralling, preparing for spring rowing. There were usually two of us Land Girls. We had to share the work, and we had about four or five cows - Shorthorns. The hay was stacked and had to be cut into flaps with a hay knife - it was hard work feeding the stock.

I had to learn the rural dialect coming from a town - Bridlington. Our dialect was not so broad. The first time I heard the shepherd shouting at his dog "Gezza wa yarn" and then "Yam it", I hadn't a clue what he was on about. One of the jobs we used to have to do was cutting turnips for sheep on the sheep fold. These were usually heaps of turnips - the cutter had to be pulled from heap to heap, the turnips forked into the cutter with a pick fork, then the handle turned. The turnips came out like chips into a scuttle. When it was full, you had to put it into troughs for the sheep to eat.

It was great when we used to have a film show at the farm. These film shows used to travel round outlying farms. I think they were just news reels - 35mm films. The film company used to put in a George Formby film or a cartoon - something for a laugh. At Cottain we had a big kitchen and all the people from the neighbouring farms would come - it was great.

I was always keen and loved to work with the horses. I often wonder now how I used to gear the horses up. I only weighed just about eight stone, but it never bothered me. We had one horse called Jet. I wasn't allowed to drive her as she had a bad habit of galloping off. She was a big animal and had to wear a collar round her neck with a chain attached to tie her up with in the stable. If you put the normal rope halter on her, she would break it. I remember going into the stable to feed the horses and Jet was in an awful state. One of the men had brought her in, tied her up and left her collar and back band braces on. She had been fighting trying to get her gear off. Her collar had worked up her head and had got fast with the collar round her neck (like a dog collar), and the back band braces were also fast. She had been pulling back and the bone above her near side eye was red raw. I went up to her but she tried to trap me on the standing. I tried several times but she wouldn't let me touch her. Anyway, I managed to get near her head and just talked to her. I don't know how long I was there but gradually I managed to get all the gear off her. Later on in the evening my boss asked who took the gear off Jet. I said "I

did". He said "Huh, I don't know how you did it, I couldn't get near her". There was no thank you, or you did well, it was all in a day's work, but I knew I'd won my spurs.

Another thing I remember at Cottain was that the eldest son was taking over another farm which his Dad had bought for him - Gasa Farm, Weaverthorpe. He set him up with implement - four horses, Jet being one of them, and some sheep. My job was to walk them from Cottain to Weaverthorpe - it must have been five or six miles. I remember it was a hot day and the flock got tired. I had to get into the middle of them and urge them on.

During harvest we had some Italian prisoners of war. Oh, they were a lazy lot! They didn't like farm work, but they were clever with their hands. They used to make string sandals with binds and twine.
I went from there to a farm near North Dalton, a much smaller farm - about 250 acres, again it was Wold land - very chalky.
There wasn't a lot to do in the evenings - for one thing, you were usually too tired. There was no such thing as overtime, but we used to go to the village hops. One group of musicians were called the "Gambling Gamblings" or the "Grembling Gemblings", they were quite good.

I used to have every other weekend off. You had to work Saturday mornings in those days, so it made a short weekend. In bad weather, I had to walk two miles from the farm downhill to the

JUNE KNAGGS ON THE RIGHT WITH SISTERS RITA IN THE BROWNIES AND PAT IN THE ARMY -1937

main road - the York-Driffield road - and wait for a bus. There were "Everingham buses", then change at Driffield, and either catch a train to Bridlington or an East Yorks bus. I remember the bus cost a shilling, a penny a mile. In fine weather I used to cycle into Driffield and leave my bike at Oldreds Garage (I don't think it's there any more).

Every season had its job. I remember before harvest cleaning out the fold yards, all done by hand. It was very hard work, and at all those jobs you got loance morning and afternoon. Its real name was allowance, not lunch, and shortened to "loance", usually cheese sandwiches or hot scones and cheese. In the afternoon it was fruit pie and tea in mugs. You never thought of washing your hands. I reckon it tasted better with all the muck on. One never ailed anything in those days.

Threshing, that was another mucky dusty job. Land Girls always got the job of chaff carrying in a big Hessian sheet. It was an awful job; when it was barley the dust used to get everywhere, and itch like mad. Your eyes used to be red raw. You always had a stick - when a shout came, a rat was running. There were always plenty of rats at the bottom of a stack. Sometimes they'd put wire netting round the stack so the rats couldn't escape - the cats and dogs had a great time.

Wet harvests were awful, especially when you had to go into the field and re-stook the stooks - that's turning each sheaf of corn round (the outside to the inside) - they never would stand right. When it was barley or oats there was always a lot of green at the bottom of the sheaf like grapes or cloves that wouldn't dry out, so on a nice fine, windy day you had to pull the stooks over with their "arses" to the wind, so the wind would blow up them and dry them.

Being a long way off a village, the lad who worked at the farm and myself used to go spuggying at night, with the aid of a torch. The sparrows used to make for the buildings at night. We used to chase them out with sticks; I know it sounds cruel nowadays, but then you didn't think anything of it. We used to go catching rabbits too with a ferret, I loved that. Then we used to do "bush beating" when the Landlord had his shoot. That was great fun too.

June Knaggs
Bridlington

I joined the Land Army whilst I was living in the Rhondda Valley, South Wales, so had no experience of country life. When called up to do something of national importance, I decided I would like to join the Land Army. It didn't really appeal to me working on a farm, so I joined the Timber Co Branch of the W.L.A. I worked in the woods chopping down trees and sawing them into pit props, also planting small trees, etc. We girls used four and a half pound axes. On joining up we had to go to a school in Carmarthen to learn about different trees - also we visited the saw mills. After our course, we passed out and were given a green beret and little brass crossed axes to fix onto our uniforms. (I still have mine).

We were also given a badge with a tree on it. Our uniforms were sent to our homes and I remember how self conscious I felt the first time I wore it.

Having arrived at the mansion, which was our billet in a small village outside Carmarthen, we had a meal then had to strip and be examined by a Doctor. The first few days I had blisters on my heels from wearing the heavy boots for our tramps through the woods, but I soon got over it.

My friend and I were soon posted to a new billet, staying with a minister and his wife. We thought we would have to be on our best behaviour and go to Chapel every Sunday. However, we had a pleasant surprise. They were very nice and treated us like members of the family. Their own children were away in the war, so I think they were pleased to have us.

Every Sunday morning Mrs Jones would bring us our breakfast in bed before she went to the Chapel. One morning she had on some very pretty ear-rings and asked if we liked them. On our saying that we did, she laughed and said "I suppose the buggers will have something to say about these" (meaning the congregation). "Never marry a minister, your life will never be your own". We were in fits of laughter.

After a while I got a transfer to a place called Talybont in Cardiganshire. They call it Dyfed now. There were two hotels in Talybont (which are still there), next door to each other - The White Lion and The Black Lion. We were billeted in The White Lion, and were well looked after by Mr and Mrs Hides. We managed to get butter and eggs and Mrs Hides used to make sandwiches for our lunch which we had in the lovely fresh air. We worked with the local men who shared their food with us. Their wives would give them extra, and considering that there was a war on, we were very lucky.

When we returned from our work one day, Mrs Hides informed us that some American G.I.s had arrived and were staying in The Black Lion next door. They had come for a few weeks' leave before being sent over to Arnhem, so they were out to enjoy themselves. After being told that there were Land Girls staying next door, they wasted no time in getting to know us. There were twins called Horace and Homer who were full of fun, and one called Ray. I was a redhead in those days, and apparently Ray had seen me walking in the woods to my work. He asked Mrs Hides "Who's the smashing redhead? Would you introduce me to her?" which she did. After that, I couldn't get rid of him. He said he wanted to marry me before he went to Arnhem and would get his C.O.'s permission. The only thing I promised was to write to him. They all used to come up to the woods where we worked, and as we felled trees they would shout "Timber". They really enjoyed themselves because, for all they knew, they may all be killed abroad.

When it was time for them to leave, all the village

was sad. They had been well liked and the children loved them. Ray didn't want to leave, but his mates managed to persuade him in the end by saying "Don't get yourself into trouble for the sake of a ruddy girl". When they pulled out they were missed for a while.

The Landlord of The Black Lion found out later that the twins Horace and Homer had been killed and Ray had been wounded and lost both legs. I suppose some of the others were lost as well. We never heard any more.

Mrs Frankland

Kent

Have you seen her?

Have you seen the Land Girl,
With her uniform complete?
And seen how very smart she looks,
So workmanlike and neat.

Or else the one whose overcoat
Is worn o'er any dress.
Land Army socks and high-heeled shoes,
T'is funny, none the less?

And people turn and look again,
"My dear, what can she be?
D'you think she's dressed up for a joke
From a funny comedy?"

So smartly wear your uniform.
Be proud that you can be
A member of that worthy force,
The Women's Land Army.

J H Summers 25319

Northants

I joined the Warwickshire W.L.A. in 1943, shortly after my eighteenth birthday. After six weeks so-called "training" in a hostel for sixty girls, six of us were chosen to be sent to a very small hostel in the village of Long Compton, which had been temporarily closed in disgrace due to the behaviour of the girls. The problem was that this hostel was next door but one to the billet of twenty G.I.s of the Signal Service Corps, who manned a small radio station at the other end of the village. The lively girls who had been there up until now had been all too friendly with their neighbours, to the extent of scandalising the village. The hostel was now to be re-opened with myself and five others espe cially chosen as being quiet, respectable types. We were lectured to this effect and warned of our responsibility. Of course we would behave, we promised. We wouldn't have anything to do with the G.I.s at all. We even joined the Youth Club run by the local Congregational Church, to show how innocuous we were.

We must have kept this up for all of three weeks. However, the charm, courtesy and easy friendliness of the American boys soon won us over, coupled with generosity we'd never dreamed of. (Well, they could afford it, couldn't they? I understand in retrospect why our own servicemen resented them so bitterly). We realised how far the rot had set in when we found ourselves rushing out from a Temperance Meeting at the Congregational Church, in time to meet the boys for a drink in the Red Lion.

Our village was (and still is) on a fairly main road, the A34, between Stratford-on-Avon and Oxford. So as well as our own "Yanks", many others would pass through in convoys of trucks and we would be thrown "goodies". I can remember thinking what on earth to do with one of my "prizes", a small packet marked "pre-mixed cereal". I suppose it was from some kind of survival kit - it didn't taste too good. Mostly, though, it was gum or chocolate, which we gratefully accepted.

Rather surprisingly, since we were poaching on her preserves, we became friendly with one of the village girls. She was the youngest of three sisters, the elder two of whom would shamelessly parade their illegitimate babies up and down the village street most afternoons, chatting up the Yanks at the same time. She told us that if we stood at a certain spot on a certain evening of the week (having procured a late pass), we would be taken to a dance at G.I. camp at Adelstrop, some miles away, and delivered home afterwards. This seemed too good to be true - but it wasn't! At the appointed time a small truck appeared, we and our village friend were hauled in, and whisked away in a hair-raising and madly exciting drive, to what seemed to us to be fairyland. In my memory, the place was a blaze of light but it couldn't have been, as the blackout regulations would never have allowed it. There was jitterbugging to a band that sounded as good as Glenn Miller, and a buffet with huge vats of butter, jam and peanut butter (among other delights) and we watched aghast as the boys spread all three in large quantities on the same piece of bread! Remember, we were all eighteen and the war was in its fifth year. We had been children when it started, and were now firmly fixed in the idea that the amount of butter to be consumed by one person in a week was limited to two ounces.

Such memories which sparked off a wave of nostalgia at the time of writing.

Mrs Erica Thomas
Rochester, Kent

I was in the W.L.A. from 1943 to 1950. I spent seven happy, hard working years, living and working from a hostel in Howden.

We did every job imaginable, and the companionship was marvellous. I particularly remember during one winter, we were sent to clear the snow off the roads. We asked 'Why can't the roadmen do it?' We were told 'Oh, the weather is too bad for them!' We often had to take the soil off the potato pies (or clamps) with picks when it was frozen.

One day, while 'heading' on the Aerodrome, we couldn't get the fire to start. With a cool head, an Airman bashed an incendiary bomb on a wall and started it for us.

There were sixty girls in the hostel. We once went on strike because we were being given mouldy food, and not much of it. Lady Dunnington Jefferson came to the hostel and gave us a good talking to. She said 'You are all mobile, you know'.

Yes, we had a lot of laughs and some heartaches, plus lots of backache! Along with the laughs we had lots of sing-songs in the fields and in the lorry going back to the hostel at the end of the day. One of the farmers used to call me 'Thrushie' after the bird. I also got called 'Little My' as there was a big Muriel too.

If I hadn't joined the W.LA. I would not have met my dear husband, who is a Latvian displaced person. He was also in a hostel run by the Agricultural Committee. We lived in a tied cottage for the first eighteen years of our married life, then my husband had a tractor accident and we moved into a council house.

His method of proposing was to lift me up, put me into the 'box' with the calves, and not let me out until I said 'Yes'.

Nowhere would you have found a better bunch of women, who never got their just deserts. A shirt and a pair of shoes was our gratuity; also a printed letter from the King.

Mrs Muriel Berzins
Aldbrough

Standing in an exposed spot in "Ten Acres" with wind whistling all around me, my hands, feet and even my nose frozen stiff, clutching an icy cabbage under each arm, I wondered just why I had chosen a Land Girl's life, when I could have been in a warm comfortable office far from the icy blast of the outside world.

Well, it was true, there was no doubting that; in fact, it was all too true. Here I was, and whatever happened I was going to make myself enjoy every minute of it and get as much out of it as I possibly could.

This strange new life, which was to be mine for over three years, started in 1943 when I first gained a little experience on a small general farm in Cobham, transferring a few months later to a poultry farm nearby. After I had been there five months, a call came for more Land Girls for dairy work, so I volunteered.

I was posted to a training farm at Limpsfield in Surrey. There were a gay crowd of girls there and, although the people in charge were not at all likeable, we managed to enjoy ourselves.

When my two months training was over, I was posted to Clammer Hill Farm which was to be my home for the next two years. Clammer Hill was about three miles from Haslemere, and the countryside around was perfect.

The farm itself was situated on top of a hill with another hill behind called "Nobby", which commanded a magnificent view; you could see for miles towards the east, and the sunrise across that stretch was a sight that I will never forget.

I had always believed that workers and farmers arose when the cock first crowed, but I was to be disillusioned for, believe me, we were up long before he ever thought of waking the countryside into life. I think our contribution was better than his, for the sound of our hob-nails on the road at five o'clock on a winter's morning roused more villagers than our fine feathered friend used to.

During the winter, our herd used to "lay-in", so were all ready in their stalls as soon as we arrived. In the summer, of course, we used to go and fetch them in from the pasture, collecting a breakfast of mushrooms on the way.

In the winter the cows have to be fed before the milking begins. Each has a pitch of hay and perhaps some mangolds. Then the good milkers are rewarded with either a measure of cow-cake or a bucket of grains. During the summer, there was no feeding to do and we could start milking them as soon as they were all chained up.

In winter and summer the actual dairy work is the same. The equipment and electric milkers have to be put together and the cows washed down. A Land Girl's work is not all honey. Imagine, on a cold frosty morning, plunging your arm up to the elbow in a pail of freezing water to reach for the cloth for washing the animals. To make matters worse, there are certain members of the tribe who, like us, object to the cold water and try to resist by suddenly kicking out at you none too gently.

We had about thirty cows in our herd, which the electric milkers would milk in about an hour. Afterwards, Florrie used to go round them to get the milk that the milkers had left. In all, the dairy work took about three hours and by that time you may be sure we were more than ready for our breakfast.

During the summer, the time between breakfast and dinner was taken up in the fields, either carting, raking or drilling etc, or perhaps hoeing or "muck" spreading. During the lay-in period in the winter, our morning was taken up in the cowsheds. Odd jobs usually came after dinner until about three o'clock when the milking would begin all over again.

Such things as cutting kale in a rainstorm, pulling frozen cabbages, back-breaking potato picking, weeding, fetching cows in the awful weather when they have grazed far down the meadows, are a few of the things that try your patience. I think kale cutting was the worst of all. Every time you strike the stem of the kale with the bill-hook or chopper, whichever you are using, you get a shower of water all over you, usually down your neck. Needless to say, you are soaked by the time the job is done.

But for all the trying times we had to bear, the beauty and glories of the spring and summer well rewarded us.

Nothing in the whole world could be more wonderful than to stand on "Nobby" and watch the sun slowly rise up from the horizon. Just to stand there and hear the birds awaken into life; the thrush who used to be always singing on the hawthorn bush; a rabbit would suddenly dart out from the hedge and back again, giving you just enough time to see the little white streak as his tail vanished. Looking up, you could see the birds all flying towards the sun. A cock would crow from somewhere in the valley, the gentle breeze would rustle in the hedgerows and trees, and from here and there the muffled lowing of the cattle from different farmsteads in the valley. Then, the most beautiful thing of all, to watch the sun rise in all its glory, spreading a mantle of golden hue right across the sky. It must be imagination, but it seems that at that moment the air seems even sweeter and everything lovelier and you yourself can feel your heart lift higher and higher every second while you gaze at that wonderful scene.

There are so many things I shall always remember, that if I went on for ever I think I could always find something new to tell.

But a few remain more vivid in my memory; "Sunbeam", who must have got so tired of my milking her, decided she wasn't having it any longer and gave me just enough time to jump off my stool before she lay down on the straw with such a sigh.

The time I stood on a plank over the heaving backs of the herd below trying to keep my balance while painting the roof of the cowshed.

Little "Twinkle", daughter of "Star", who though only one week old used to have great fun running from one end of the shed to the other along the gutter, slow up about two yards from the wall, slide on all fours, bump into the wall and lie in a heap panting and puffing, only to get up in a few seconds to do the whole thing over again.

The young bull-calf that sent me flying when I was feeding him. He made a dash for freedom out into the open and it took me an hour to chase him all down the meadows. I never caught him; it was only with careful manoeuvring and "sweet" words that I got him back into the yard and left him to the farmer.

The night we were awakened by the thundering of hooves and on arriving at the farm found the whole herd, absolutely mad, thundering round and round "Nobby". All the gates leading to their pastures had been closed and they could not escape. The reason for their frenzy was soon to be seen, for somebody had set light to the observation hut on the very top of the hill and the flames had scared the animals.

My favourite corner of Muddy Lane where primroses grew amongst the ferns and in the hedge "Hoppy", my robin friend, reared his family.

Also the farm cats who used to get an extra dish of milk when no-one was around.

Then the time I was kicked off my stool by two young heifers, one after the other, and landed in the manger looking up to see two mournful faces staring at me.

The time I forgot to put a churn under the cooler and all the milk gaily ran away onto the dairy floor.

Also, when washing the dairy utensils, I tipped a bucket of water into a churn to swill it round and, to my horror, the churn was full of milk.

Poor old Whiskey, a black and white Friesian, who had T.B. on the brain and after days of care and patience was found dead one morning when we arrived at the farm.

Victoria, the tyrant of the herd, who was always where she shouldn't be; always far down the other end of the pastures when calling the cows in for milking. She always had to be fetched and, after walking about half a mile through the fields to fetch her, would wait until I was up to within two yards of her and then she would charge away to trot merrily up to the fields to join her sisters who had already reached the farm.

The awful feeling when the alarm rang and you were snug and warm between cosy sheets, knowing soon you would be out in all the fury of pouring rain and driving wind.

Then there was "Edie", our Cockney Land Girl, who thought that if she sang rude songs to the cows they would give more milk. She kept the whole farm alive with her chatter of latest romances, which included one from almost every race on earth. When she left us it was "Salvie", her Italian. Our greatest laugh came when she rushed out to me to say "There's a smasher in the cow sheds". The "smasher" turned out to be the rather masculine lady vet who visited the farm.

Then last, but not least, Jolly and Hobber, the cart horses, who used to get an extra measure of oats when the farmer was not around and who were my friends on lots of day journeys to the Blacksmiths. Those were the days when I used to get a "leg-up" onto Jolly's broad back, a final check up for sandwiches and thermos, and we were off. Steadily plodding our way down the lanes, across timber plantations and fields, over streams, up and down hills until we came to our destination.

Sometimes Dolly, the milk float pony, used to accompany us, but we were better alone for she used to make Jolly nervous. I had a lot of trouble once getting Jolly past a steam-roller, and then it was only with the help of the road men that we managed to get him past by pushing him backwards past the steaming monster. I used to love my visits to Thomas the Blacksmith. Sandwiches were eaten in my favourite spot underneath the chestnut tree as soon as I arrived and the horses were put to graze for an hour. Then, when work was started, I used to help Thomas with the bellows - a job from which I got a lot of fun. Thomas was a man of few words - his vocabulary consisted of two words - "Yes" and "No". He used to love to get you talking and all he would say was "Yes - yes - yes", drawling the words slowly, and "No - no - no", during the little stories that I would tell him. The only time he used to vary his speech was when I worked the bellows for him and then it was "Slowly - slowly - slowly - steady - a little faster - whoa - whoa - that's it, Missey, enough now". His forge was over 300 years old, just the same and no alterations since it was built. He used to be very proud of it too. The same family had been working there since it was first used.

When all was finished, a leg-up, a wave goodbye, and we would be off, the end of a lovely day.

One of the most beautiful memories of my farming days occurred during the harvest. We had help up from the village and, in all, there were about fifteen of us, including the farmer and his son, the two other Land Girls, myself and old and young men from the village.

About 7.30 pm our picnic supper was brought down to the fields by the farmer's wife and his daughter. Jugs of cocoa, thick sandwiches, cakes, buns and scones, all made by the farmer's wife, and as tasty as they could be. I do not think I can ever remember eating food with such gusto as when we had our picnic suppers.

We had eaten our fill and each returned to our various positions - the farmer to his pitching, Ralph to his tractor, the other girls, Florrie and Winnie, to their pitching and I, a heave up, and I was onto one of the wagons to start building yet another load.

That night there was a beautiful harvest moon, the sun sank and the shadows fell, and the moon rose higher and higher, and still we went on steadily until nearly midnight when the last loads were finished. The men threw up ropes, secured the loads, and all the waggons and helpers started to wend their way back to the farm. Mr Perritt called and asked me if I wanted to stay on the load for a ride back. His offer was gratefully accepted.

It had been very hot all day, and the night was warm. I lay down in the warm corn and relaxed. All I could see was the heavens filled with stars and, dominating them all, the harvest moon. A faint breeze fanned my face and seemed to refresh me more than a night's rest could ever have done. The gentle jolting of the waggon beneath me could have rocked me to sleep, but I was too happy to sleep. I lay there absolutely contented, full of thankfulness for the inspiration that made me come to this glorious life, and knowing that the beauty that was all around me was put there for everyone and could be found by anyone who cared to look for it.

Audrey Harvey

Harvest Home

You are my harvest home, the last rich sheaf
My tired arms shall gather to my heart.
Long are the days from snowy winter seed-time
When we ploughed, harrowed and drilled the dormant grain.

Long are the days through biting winds of March,
April's laughing showers and May's sweet green.
June's bright hours and blazing days of summer,
With the haze shimmering from the sunparched land;
And the silver hay piled high in scended loads.
Oh, the long days of July,
Dusty August and her dragging toil,
'Til with a mighty shout came gay September.
And the sheaves ranged in their four square shocks,
The carts creaking and the horses straining;
With our hearts spurring our arms to beat the sun.

The fields are quiet now the corn is carted,
The harvest moon dreams on the empty land.
On the bulging sacks where the quick mice dart,
And I am free to cry "Te Deum" with my hand in yours.
My tired arms may gather to my heart, this last rich sheaf:
You are my harvest home.

E.M.B.
October 1944

54

I joined the W.L.A. when I was 19 years old, having lived in London.

It was a cold afternoon in November 1942 when I arrived in Braintree, Essex, to start my service in the W.L.A. I had a battered old suitcase secured with a leather belt and two paper carrier bags which held all my luggage. We were billeted with a very nice family. They had two sons, Cecil and Wilfred, and our job was threshing - hard work, but we enjoyed it. However, all work and no play soon caught up with us - we wanted some variety! At this time we couldn't get to any of the dances at the U.S. bases because the farmer we were billeted with was very strict on time. One night in particular we thought we would go for a walk to post some letters which we normally posted during the day in little pillar boxes in the village. We heard music - it was black all around but we groped our way along the road and came upon this pub. When we opened the door we found it was full of Yanks. We forgot all about time, and when we got back to the house we were locked out. After a lot of fuss, the farmer's wife let us in but the next day we went to H.Q. at Chelmsford and complained how we were treated.

They gave us a transfer and we lived with another family, much younger - they understood that we wanted some variety. We were working hard and entitled to some fun. We made up for it - after Christmas in early 1943 came a huge number of G.I. flyers. I met Sergeant Blair Allenbaugh who was stationed at Great Saling. He flew a B26 Marauder and along with my friends we had great times. I look back at those wonderful times - my memories are so vivid! When I hear Glenn Miller's music I'm there again, just carried away.

Florence Montgomery,
Gwent, South Wales

I served in the Women's Land Army from 2 November 1942 to December 1944. I was twenty years old and had previously done clerical work.

My first posting was onto a farm about four miles from Appleby, Westmorland. The old homestead was in ruins and the big house (Hall) was occupied by an old lady and her daughter, who was about thirty five years old. It had once been lived in by the gentry, but there must have been quite a lot of neglect over the years. The entrance I used led into a boiler room (boiler not working) full of sacks of animal feed. The kitchen where meals were served was littered with little piles of cinders covering up cat dirt. I had a large bedroom with a chair, a single bed, a small chest of drawers and a lamp. There was a servant's stair case that led to my bedroom from the boiler room.

The first month was a training period! When the Land Army Rep came to see me, she told me that I was the eighteenth Land Girl these people had had. She would be in close contact with me and try to improve conditions.

The farm boasted a pedigree Shorthorn Herd, and a bull weighing a ton. Even in those days they recorded the work done on the farm that the daughter and I did (no male labour). They used the bull; while I held the cow or heifer the daughter dealt with the bull. I remember being told to put my thumb and first finger up the heifer's nose and nip (poor thing). One day the bull rode the heifer into thick mud. Meanwhile my wellingtons had stuck, so I stepped out of them right into the mud while letting go of the heifer. I squeezed up against the wall and shut my eyes while the bull went sailing past!!!

So much for the training. I was given a bucket with some cow nuts in the bottom and a halter, then told to go and catch the horse. (This was before daylight - you can imagine what I felt like). There were two horses charging round me, and I didn't bring one of them home the first morning but Miss F made sure I did every morning after! I can understand why the previous Land Girl shut the daughter (Miss F) in with the bull before she left.

I stayed six weeks and it seemed like six months.

Kendal was my home and every afternoon I got my bike out and pedalled like mad to catch the bus, dumping my bike on Orion Fell (in the hedge). I was supposed to finish at 12 noon,, the bus left at 1.45 pm. I was always late finishing - the excuse was they'd just rung Appleby to find out what time it was.

The farm was quite isolated and the postman was the only visitor. He had the job of wringing the necks of sick hens.

I lived on another farm for six weeks and never had an egg. The few eggs they got went to the packing station. So much marg and butter was taken from my rations for cooking (scones) and I was given one jar of jam (ration for a month). As we had jam at breakfast and tea, mine did not last the month! Every Saturday my family sent me back with one jar of homemade jam.

Yes, the first six weeks in the Women's Land Army I'll never forget.

Mrs E Christian
Lancaster

I served in the W.L.A. from May 1943 to September 1946, and believe me it was the loveliest and most exciting time in my life, but it's time the general public knew about our contribution to World War II.

My most vivid memory is of Spring 1945 hoeing onions in a 200 acre field and the sky was full every morning, as far as the eye could see, of B29 bombers going to Germany - the noise overhead was so tremendous the other girls and I had to use sign language to communicate with each other.

I was billeted in the Village Hall, a large imposing house called "Wrangle Hall" in a village called Wrangle situated seven miles from Boston, fourteen miles from Skegness, Lincolnshire. I was one of thirty two Yorkshire girls stationed there. We were looked after by a matron, cook, and several house maids. Coming from a terraced house in a street I thought I was in another world. Talk about posh! I became a much more cultured person.

Six of us worked for a gentleman farmer (R. C. Boswer) who owned thousands of acres. We only met the foreman who gave us our orders every day - occasionally we saw the farmer flash by the fields in his Jaguar.

We worked from dawn to dusk in the summer, dressed in shorts and suntop and acquiring a glorious sun tan. As you can imagine, we would wow all the men we met at dances, etc.

I get mad when people assume we were always messing about in the haystacks with the farm workers who were exempt from the armed services. It was not so - they were too mystic and ignorant, a hundred years behind us, still touching their forelocks to the foreman.

The winters were very hard, picking sprouts covered in icicles, chopping tops off sugar beet, standing on top of haystacks threshing, the backs of our hands always bleeding as gloves got wet straight away. We got to be very skilled working with huge shire horses (Percherons) as well as the land work.

Land Girls were the only people in the country who were entitled to double rations.

The old people in the village were very nice to us but the young girls were very spiteful towards us. They always worked at the other end of the field - consequently we felt compelled to beat them in speed at whatever job we were doing. We weren't welcome in the village pub.

The vicar visited us once a week to give whoever wanted confirmation lessons; also a nice nurse came once a month to examine our hair for lice. We were all provided with a bike and a War Ag. man came every week to mend punctures, etc.

HMS "Royal Arthur" was based at Skegness so

hundreds of sailors were around, also hundreds of airmen at the dances - we were overwhelmed with invitations to dances. RAF officers and Navy officers were not allowed to consort with W.A.A.F. and W.R.E.N.S. in the ranks - but as we were a voluntary organisation they would consort with us, so our boyfriends were bomber crews, officers - Class!

As for the Yanks, Boston and Peterborough were swarming with them - they were better dressed than our officers. We danced with them and they taught us all to jive! Contrary to public opinion, we always found them perfect gents, not sex mad, but always seemed to be eager to marry us after several dates, especially Yorkshire girls! I always backed off when the courtship seemed to be getting serious as I knew I could never leave my Mum, Dad, brothers and sisters. Of course I never envisaged the time would come when one could fly home in a day otherwise, with hindsight, I think I would have married one of the several I fell in love with. They were very generous with gifts of chocolate, cigs, and pure silk stockings. Our matron allowed us to invite them to Wrangle Hall for tea and refreshments and listen to records played on the gramophone.

For each six months we served we were given a red cloth half diamond to sew on our greatcoats. The next one received was sewn to the other to form a diamond. I finished with three and a half diamonds on my coat - that way one could see how long a girl had been a Land Girl. By the way,

in 1947 I married an English sailor, till then "Virgo Intacta".

I was indeed fortunate to experience such a great my life.

Madge Humphries,
Mexborough, South Yorkshire

The Women's Land Army commenced for me in May 1943. I travelled from Bradford to Lincoln. In those days it took a long time, changing at Doncaster with a long wait because it was wartime. I arrived at Lincoln, had two hours waiting time, and so went to a cinema with other Land Army girls I had travelled with. The film was Phantom Of The Opera (with Claude Rains). It was frightening. Then we caught the train to the village of Sascilly, a very active place. We had to do eight weeks training there - market gardening, forestry, crops, general farm work, milking, mucking out animals, taking water into fields for animals, nettle cutting in fields (there was a law they should be kept down) and hedging sides of the roads.

In the village the chapels gave social evenings, concerts and musical evenings, dances, and the latest dance music of Glenn Miller. Everyone was friendly - all the shops gave you a hello when you bought their goods.

When we had time we caught the train or the R.A.F. service bus into Lincoln. There we were allowed to go into the servicemen's and women's pubs. Here we exchanged fruit for chocolate with R.A.F., American, Canadian, and Polish airmen of many ranks. Then back at the village we would attend local get-togethers with service men and women. At the activities we had to wear Land Army uniform which was, as you know, fine khaki breeches, cream shirt, green tie, and brown heavy tie shoes well kept, and a dark great-coat. We felt great because everyone wore uniform.

All these dances and social evenings were attended by English, American, Canadian and Polish air crew and airmen. These men flew dangerous air missions and some would never return back to base. We girls became very friendly with these men. We were young and romantic, and we wanted to send them away with a little love and kisses. Some wanted more, but that was up to the individual. We had our friends back at our billet which was a beautiful old mansion type house taken over by the Government. We all had bunk beds, kitchen facilities, and a room where we could have friends and cups of tea. Food of course was in short supply, but we all

managed. We talked, laughed and played Glenn Miller records, and perhaps we would go to the local cinema in Lincoln once a month. We would count the 'planes when they set out at night and hear them return in the mornings too. It made us sad when we knew that some would never return. I was eventually posted to the village of Kirton Lindsey, again a small place. I was issued with a Raleigh bicycle by the Government. I had a three mile ride to a farm of sixty acres. It was a busy little farm and I drove two lovely shire horses - Blanom and Jolly. They were attached to a large wooden dray cart.

I did all general farm work but I forgot to tell you we had beautiful orchards. I pulled apples and stored them all in rows in a keeping room. I ate with the farmer at breakfast time, him with his ham and me with my farm bread.

Each day a military truck would drop about ten prisoners of war to work in the fields and the farmer would let me work with them on my own. I was worried at first, but they behaved themselves very well indeed and it was alright. Some of these men were not used to manual work, some were naval officers, Italians, Germans. Their hands would bleed and I bandaged them; they were human beings and, like us, did not want a war.

On days off Scunthorpe was our nearest town. I have been a life long member of The Salvation Army, and I remember the Scunthorpe people opened their homes to all servicemen and women. What great respect the Scunthorpe people had for the band marching down Main Street. Forty four men all very smart.

All this happened in my Land Army days. What *lovely* memories.

Mrs Muriel May Jagger

Calf's Lament

My name is Pat, I am a calf
My Land Girl often makes me laugh.
The way she thinks she knows just how
To bring me up to be a cow.

Why won't she let me eat all day,
And guzzle luscious meadow hay?
Or fill my tummy up with swede?
Life should consist of one long feed.

Outside this yard I'd like to run,
To chase a hen would be such fun.
She seems to think I'd do some harm
Investigating round the farm!

Thank heaven for the day-to-be,
When all my grief shall turn to glee.
For when she milks me in a pail,
I'll love to lash her with my tail!

M Baxter 62953
W Kent

Iserved for four and a half years in the Land Army, and was stationed at Hanimoor, Sturminster, Newton, Dorset, at a hostel for twenty girls. We had a housekeeper called Miss Arnold, and had money deducted from our wages for board and laundry which left us very little cash for ourselves. We had to pay full price for everything, no N.A.A.F.I. for us like the other services. Also, when we disbanded, no cash in hand or clothes like the other services received. It seems that we are the "Forgotten Army". We are not even included in the March Past on November 11. But looking back, they were great days. I made good friends and really liked the work.

The hours we worked varied with whatever was to be done. We did two and a half hours before breakfast at seven thirty, which was fried potatoes or sausage and beans. Sometimes we had a real treat, like a boiled egg. We never had a choice; whatever was on the table, we ate.

Potato picking was back aching work, as was digging sugar-beet out of frosted ground. We gathered brussel sprouts, cut cabbage, and dug carrots out of the ground. We used to sink into the soil when it was very wet, and trying to pull ourselves out was a task on its own. We milked the cows night and morning, even white-washed the cowshed walls at the end of winter.

Summer brought a lot of work - planting corn and barley seed, and muck spreading, which was done by filling a wheelbarrow with a fork, then wheeling it to wherever on the field it had to be put. Hoeing weeds in the vegetable fields, which seemed to go on for miles. Threshing was a very dusty job. Girls would be forking the cornstakes up to the feeder, the feeder cut string on the cornstakes and then fed it into the machine. This used to rock, and all you hoped was that you didn't fall in. The corn came out of the machine into sacks which girls used to replace when full. Covered in dust, we were a sorry sight at the end of the day. We trimmed hedges around the fields and even repaired stone walls - we were Jacks of all trades.

Some farmers were decent to us, making tea for our lunch and tea breaks, as we all took sandwiches; but some farmers wouldn't even let us have hot water to make our own tea. We had to go to the cow sheds and get cold water from the tap to drink.

We had our laughs, though. One girl while muck spreading fell right onto the pile. You can imagine the sight she was - we all fell about laughing. We worked with Italian prisoners and one used to shout to me "Eileen, I love you". My reply was "Roberto, I hate the sight of you". One day, our feet sunk into the ground and the farmer came up on a big white horse. I explained that the soil was too wet to work. His reply was "My feet are not dirty". I told him to get off his horse and they soon would be. I got into trouble for that, lost a week's wage, but still had to pay for board and laundry. The W.L.A. got nothing cheap. Another time I had to take the bull to the cow.

The silly bull missed the cow and I got everything over me. That caused many a laugh for weeks.

Some Saturdays we finished work at twelve o'clock which gave us time to get away for the weekend. My mate and I used to cycle to Blandford, leaving the bikes at a pub, and whilst waiting for the bus home we used to meet the G.I. nurses. They were a lovely crowd of girls and some weekends, instead of going home, the nurses took us to the G.I. Hospital where we visited the sick lads. Most of them were badly wounded and were waiting to be sent home.

There was an American camp by us and we used to meet the G.I.s in the local pub. We had sing songs around a battered piano, and drank cider as beer was very short on supply. Sometimes we went to their camp to dance. We really enjoyed ourselves - especially the food they had prepared for us. It was like another world. There was not much entertainment in the country, and we would go with the G.I.s to the cinema which was in Blandford. They would sneak a lorry out to take us amid great excitement hoping the M.P.s wouldn't catch the driver. I bought two khaki silk shirts off them. They were heaven to wear after our issued thick shirts.

I had a G.I. boyfriend called Fred, and I also saw another one at Weymouth called Bob. One night when I was out with Fred, he got a bit out of hand. I gave him a smack and he landed in a ditch full of water (some smack). As luck had it, he saw the funny side and was always a decent guy towards me ever afterwards. He would give me sweets, stockings and cigs. I even got a real silk shirt from him, which was better to wear than the Land Army ones.

I must say though, that to hear the G.I.s talk, they all had good jobs back home and lived in big white houses. Some girls believed them, then got a shock after marrying them, going to the States and finding it was all lies. After saying that, some did find happiness.

Bob and I used to go to the pictures mostly and sometimes I would take him home for a meal. I remember one weekend my mate had given Fred my address and I came home with Bob. There sat Fred being entertained by my Mother. I managed to calm both down, but I don't know how I talked myself out of that one. I always was a dare-devil and still am - life's too short to be miserable.

One thing I shall always remember about the G.I.s is their dancing, jiving and rock and roll. We had a ball of a time with them.

I left the W.L.A. in 1945. I damaged my back by falling off a rick onto a haycart. It was a year before real trouble started and, by then, too late to claim from the W.L.A. I have had five major operations on my spine, but live each day happily. Like me, lots of ex W.L.A. girls are full of rheumatism and are now paying for getting wet through in the fields and letting our uniform dry on us.

Mrs E R Barrow, *Liverpool*

I was a member of the W.L.A. from April 1943 and was released in February 1946. I was so bored in Civvy Street, I rejoined in September 1946 and left after my marriage in 1948.

Of course I knew G.I.s during my stay. I was working on a farm near Tiverton, Devon. Several thousand Americans were stationed there so, like most other girls, I had a G.I. for a boyfriend. I remember his surname was Maxwell "Not Maxwell House coffee you know", he said. I hadn't a clue what he meant then. I'd only heard of Camp coffee. Generally I think they looked on our job with amusement. I know one was surprised to see blisters on my hands (I'd been doing a lot of hoeing just then). "Gosh sakes, honey, you really do have to work on that farm". I felt quite pleased, he thought that I passed it off by saying "Just for King and Country". The Americans used to call after us and ask "What does W.L.A. stand for, honey?" Usually we'd reply "We Love Americans", the answer they expected to hear. Some said "Willing Little Angels!" or "We Love Airmen" or "We Lie Around". It was an exciting time for us and I look back to the W.L.A. with great pleasure.

Later, I went to Bristol and lived in a Hostel. I went to different farms each day doing field work. Sometimes we worked on commons that were cultivated because of the war, going out in gangs with a foreman in charge. Usually it was an Irishman named Joe. Although he later married a Land Girl, I don't think he thought much of us as workers. He grumbled at us for not offering to work overtime. Two girls had the previous week, after tax. One girl had 3d extra, the other 8d. He argued that it would do us more good than "lying on our backs at night in the grass!" He nearly choked when one of us suggested we could earn more money that way.

When we were out in gangs like this, to spend a penny we had to wander off, usually in twos, to a quiet spot out of view, or so we thought. I remember feeling really embarrassed because when he was annoyed over something with my friend and me, he finished up by telling us off and then said he'd "seen us with our arses to the wind". We didn't know where to look!

Mrs Jean Retmanski
Bedworth, Warwickshire

y name is Terry (Therese) and I joined the W.L.A., aged 17 years and 3 months, in 1942, much against the wishes of my parents who had visions of me donning my cap and gown in the hallowed halls of Girton, Cambridge, where I had attained an exhibition scholarship from my very good convent school. Since the academic life didn't appeal at the time and all my friends were joining up, so did I! I think my Father might have viewed this rebellion with less languor had I gravitated towards the W.R.N.S. (Navy), since he himself had been a Lieutenant in the Royal Navy - but I was too young for anything except the W.L.A., so that seemed to be that! This is just to set the picture, you understand. I had my interview, was accepted - all the gear started to arrive at my home - such hilarity that uniform engendered - cord khaki breeches, thick green sweater, cream shirts, green tie, dungarees, 'bum' warmer overcoat and that HAT, strong walking shoes and boots complete with studs and steel heelplates. Since I loved clothes, I viewed all this lot with a very jaundiced eye, but being tall, blonde and slim, once assembled on my person they didn't look half bad - quite fetching, in fact - my Father even took a snapshot.

Came the day of departure - loads of instructions about staying 'pure', men were devils in disguise (from Mum) and you'll be home in six weeks (from Dad), and off I tootled on my first train journey alone to Wrexham in North Wales where I was to have the six weeks training (imagine - six weeks for a convent-bred townie who didn't know one end of a cow from another!) Those six weeks were pure HELL! Accustomed to somewhat better accommodation - the hostel was a shock - sleeping in a bunk, mediocre food - twenty more homesick girls like me - and the work was killing. Blistered feet and hands - rising at 6.30 each morning, work starting at 7.30. Picking beetroot was my first job - the sight of a never-ending sea of beetroot was mind boggling. (I thought it came in jars!) The introduction to cows I shall never forget - the mucking out was first, followed by squeezing those dreadful teats which refused to yield a single drop of milk (I thought it came in bottles) until one's fingers seized up and turned blue. AND, they kicked sideways, and very good they were too - finding just the right spot where one was sitting. Potato picking and mangold pulling were guaranteed to wrench the spine, so one developed a sort of hunched posture - trying to straighten out was AGONY. In any case, each night I wept buckets - determined to go home next day - but of course never did. The vision of Dad wagging a finger and saying "I told you so" was more than pride would allow.

When those dreadful weeks ended, off we all scattered, in my case to a hostel of forty girls in North Wales. Beautiful country, terrible people! I was the only English girl and the youngest, and conversation in Welsh was maintained with relish. The matron was a tub-thumping Baptist spinster with psychopathic tendencies and hated me on sight. All that long blonde hair, lipstick and mounds of luggage she took in at one glance -

not to say ENGLISH- and it was war from the start. Since we could wear civilian clothes off duty, my quite extensive wardrobe had travelled with me. This turned out to be something of an asset since I could 'lend out' various bits and pieces and increase my somewhat lowly standing into something approaching being finally accepted.

My assessment by the local War Agricultural Committee was favourable. The 'labour officer' was young, quite dishy and English, and since I was quite pretty, and batted the old eyelashes and flashed the teeth at him quite a lot, I was assigned to 'machinery section'. TRACTORS, all the things pulled by tractors, and MOTORS. I was taught to drive everything and after a few weeks passed my driving test (theirs) and was allocated a small Hillman Utility truck to help out with ferrying the hostel girls to far-flung hill farms. How I shudder now - thinking of screeching round those mountain roads knowing almost nothing about roads or driving in the sense we do today.

I did all the usual farm jobs, threshing, harvesting, mucking out cowsheds, tables, pig sties, and *very, very* gradually became (in all modesty) quite good at most things, and actually started to enjoy it.

The social life was fairly negligible - small country town - one cinema, one village hall with a 'hop' on Saturday evenings, and seven pubs. The local blokes didn't appeal, but mercifully we had an ACK-ACK battery nearby and the soldiers there were a God- send. I became friendly with the C.O. and he became very useful when hefty arms were needed around the hostel. They were allowed by 'her' to visit two evenings per week - thrown out at ten o'clock on the dot, when we were then expected to bed down until the bell rang at six-thirty am to start another day. Since it was a one-storey building, bunking out through windows after ten o'clock was commonplace although coping with the 'black-out' blinds proved to be a bit tricky - especially getting back in again once one's bit of romance reached its finale. Being something of a madam I 'bunked out' frequently and would join my gallant captain for snorts in the mess and invariably met various fellow sinners there. This is where I tasted my first alcoholic drink and hated it, but it did give a buzz and no mistake! The bad head at six thirty am was another story! No-one slept around in those days - at least I didn't, perhaps some did but kept very quiet about it.

The farmers and farms were variable. Our 'boss' tried to be fair, allocating rotten farms in rotation, and some of those hill farms were putrid - no sanitation, dirty, and the farmers were like nothing I'd ever come across - hardly civilised. One in particular springs to mind - an old farmer with two sons - no woman to cope, and their place was christened 'Wuthering Heights'. The sons were strong, good looking, illiterate and had the habits of the pigs they reared. Since it was very isolated when help was needed I had to take the truck along with an older Welsh speaking colleague and do the necessary. Much of our time was spent cleaning the farmhouse, which was unspeakably filthy, and one time the old chap got ill and took to his bed and Muriel (certainly not me) bathed him, changed his nightshirt and the bed linen before we could summon a Doctor. There was no telephone, so a son had to fetch the doctor in a pick-up truck. Muriel was a gem - I watched her cope for days with awe-stricken admiration - we didn't dare mention all this at the hostel. We were land workers, not home helps. I wondered often in that desolate place what my Father would have thought had he seen us in action. Eventually, of course, the old man recovered and we were removed hastily by the War Agricultural Committee, the Doctor having told everyone how magnificently we had coped there.

At another hill farm I caught impetigo from an isolation hospital, covered in gentian violet and taking daily a horde of bug-ridden evacuee children (from Liverpool, which was being heavily bombed), also covered in gentian violet, all with cropped heads and scabies, for a trek through the Welsh hills. Since it was desolate I didn't mind, and later saw the film 'Inn of the Sixth Happiness' with Ingrid Bergman trekking across China with her tatty retinue - and everything flooded back.

Italian prisoners were a hazard - plenty of them in Wales, and whatever it was they were supposed to put in their tea, certainly

didn't have much effect. One never dared turn one's back - and an accidental meeting in a loft or barn meant a fight almost to the death - how we thanked the good Lord for those stout breeches! I suppose looking back it was all a bit of a lark - some of those W.O.P.S. were incredibly handsome, and added a bit of spice to the mundane working day. The fact that most were bone idle, hated Mussolini (or so they said) and were terrified of Australian soldiers was academic - they seemed to enjoy being prisoners and actually taught me to sing 'O Sole Mio' in Italian, a mark in their favour.

Getting back to hostel life - my captain had wangled a radiogram from some N.A.A.F.I. or other and we started our own little social

THERESE (TERRY) RIGBY MORGAN 1945

evenings. SHE didn't approve and blamed me, and thought Glenn Miller music was decadent in the extreme. I started a social committee with myself as secretary and in a fit of enthusiasm wrote an article about poor, unrecognised, lonely, forgotten Land Army Girls, and sent it off to the Field magazine where it was subsequently published. After a few weeks of circulation, all HELL broke loose. Mountains of mail started to arrive, all addressed to me - articles appeared from everywhere - gramophones, games, books, musical instruments - talk about Pandora's Box - the Field was much more lethal! Even intrepid old me started to get alarmed - girls couldn't get back from work quickly enough to view the day's accumulation and SHE was reduced to a screaming wreck.

Needless to say, I was hauled before the War Agricultural Committee, told what a troublemaker I was, and SACKED! Sent off home in disgrace, summoned to Headquarters shortly after, and was promptly informed I was to be given my own hostel in East Anglia. Apparently they thought I was original and imaginative and could control, even though I was not yet nineteen years old.

Terry Morgan
Lancashire

I lived at Hull when my papers came to go into the W.L.A. Poor Mum ran to Grandma's and said "She's going foreign" - I suppose Wales seemed a long way in those days.

Once there I found that most people spoke Welsh which made me very home-sick at first, but I didn't want to leave after having gone through my training.

The first time that I did the milking, there were more tears in the bucket than milk and I thought my wrists had broken. I really wanted to go into Yorkshire, but the powers that be said that I must stay in Wales and put me near Chester with a nice Lady called Mrs Wilton who still sends me Christmas cards.

A Welsh friend of mine worked with me at Joby Jones' farm and we had to shout down a trumpet he carried about with him.

The muck spreading was very hard, and I often wondered how we got through the winter.

We had lots of laughs, and I remember one morning Joby said that I had to go cocking down the field with Billy. You can imagine the looks that passed between us. Being told to turn a handle whilst Joby shaved the cows' tails gave us another laugh. My Mum used to say that my letters home were a tonic, but you certainly learnt about life pretty fast when you worked with animals.

I couldn't get home very often, and my friend Doreen would take me along to her house for the weekend. One weekend we were late back, and Joby gave Doreen the sack. I said that I would go too and that's how we came to be at dear Queensbridge Hostel, where the girls were a great crowd. If we worked a way off the hostel, we went by jeep and oh! how we used to sing!

Learning to ride those awful War Department bikes with a crossbar wasn't very pleasant. We often fell off into something soft!! I spent a lot of time teaching my London friend Sheila to ride. She says she has never looked at another since.

I went to one lovely farm where they said "Throw your sandwiches to the pigs and have dinner with us!" The daughter played Ink Spots records to us all dinnertime. When I hear the old records now the memories certainly come flooding back.

I'll never forget the lovely dances in the village hall. Our Warden often invited the troops for sing-songs and parties round the piano. It was a lovely old house that we lived in, and we brought it to life.

How my dear Mum got my washing clean I don't know. I would pack it into a box with a bit of butter or anything the farmer gave me. It must have been a good help to Mum, as the rations were few and far between. We never saw fruit in the hostel, so

Mum sometimes sent me a jar of jam - lovely.

We were very proud of our uniforms, especially when we had a parade with the other forces, and marched along with our heads held high. I lost most of my clothes in the bombing of Hull, so I was glad of my uniform.

Mrs W Kidd
Beverley

Ghosts (Hereford)

I passed by cornfields golden in the morning sun,
Orchards with apples ripe upon the trees.
Later I viewed the river from the old stone bridge,
And ghosts of war time friends stood with me in the evening breeze.

I climbed the slope to Redhill Railway Bridge,
Strolled gently down through Grafton Lane.
I glimpsed the distant trees of Dinedor Hill,
And ghosts walked with me in the summer rain.

I walked in morning sunshine on the castle green,
Crossed the old suspension bridge above the Wye.
To the lawns and meadows, through the avenue of limes,
And the ghosts were there, accompanying my sigh.

St Martin's Church with yew trees seemed the same,
The once familiar chapel was hidden from view.
I walked within the cathedral's hallowed walls,
At morning service, ghosts still shared the pew.

I met old friends who still remembered me,
Looking for wild flowers on my way.
I shed a tear for all those wartime friends,
For they were young, but I am old and grey.

Dorothy Hodgkinson

I wasn't old enough to join up during World War 2, but volunteered for the W.L.A. in March 1946 until its "winding up" in November 1950, doing most of my stay in Wainfleet, Lincolnshire, and enjoying ALL of it! I must be of peasant stock!

Many years after, I learned of one Harland Tracey, a G.I. from "our" local village of Goxhill, who was sent to Wainfleet to man a tracking station - in a field belonging to my old friend Bill's Dad! Evidently when the G.I.s wanted to use their equipment, they would wave a towel, signalling Bill to stop tractoring, please, as the tractor noise spoiled their equipment's performance (talk about Dad's Army!)

Harland loved Wainfleet - off duty he would pop into the local pub to be with the folks! I never met him, but through another ex RAF friend we got in touch and he sent me photos of himself (Duke) and his dear wife Margaret (Queen!) and tapes with some memories and lots of music from their local radio station in Maine, U.S.A. Margaret always maintained that Harland would have "won" an English Rose had he not been married!

After his death a year or so ago, I asked her for a photograph of him in uniform in World War II- this was duly sent, with her love - the original had been taken here in Grimsby!

I was an occasional guest at Goxhill Officers Club - this was during the war. We were made very welcome there, and the food was excellent! The Yanks were very concerned over our tiny rations (their way of saying it!). They were almost all very well mannered and attentive.

Apart from the horror, a wartime growing up in a port like Grimsby was a great experience. We had every nationality here - the best education one could have!

Peg Francis
Grimsby

I was eighteen when I joined the W.L.A. and I can say with all honesty that they were the best years of my life.

I was in Wales at a little place called Cross Ash, with twenty eight other girls from around the country; Leeds, Manchester, Liverpool, Wakefield, Cambridge, Newport and Cardiff to name but a few. My best friend was Laura. She had red hair which matched my auburn locks, and we got along famously.

In the winter we found it hard to get up early and go out into the frost-covered fields which were often so thick with fog that you couldn't see a hand in front of you. We looked forward to getting back to the hostel, having tea, then sitting in front of the fire just reading or chatting amongst ourselves. Often we would dance, especially when the Airmen from Hereford came to see us. We also knew French Airmen, but could not converse with them like we could with the Americans and Tommies. There were a lot of Army people stationed near us and we went to the Y.M.C.A. dances on Friday nights, knowing that we had to walk twelve miles back to the hostel, come rain or shine, but not minding a bit after the smashing time we'd had.

Transport was few and far between in out-lying country villages and we Land Girls often had to rely on hitching a ride. Our village only had two buses a day, one in the morning and one at night, and I remember one weekend my friend and I decided to go home for the weekend. Missing the bus, we had to thumb a lift and shortly a Landrover pulled up. The English driver said "Hop in the back, girls". My heart stopped when we saw six Germans sitting there. Two of them were Generals, but they spoke to us in broken English and showed us photos of their families. The Generals never worked, but went around the farms overseeing the Germans that did.

Once we saw a German being taken for a walk by an English soldier outside the grounds of Nevill Hall hospital. He shook his fist and spat at us, so our soldier punched him and gave him a push to help him on his way.

Life had its lighter side, and sometimes when we were working the potato fields the training planes would fly really low dropping notes asking us to meet the boys at Hereford.

Haymaking was a hard but gay time, and we would work from eight in the morning until ten or eleven at night but it was great in the sun working in shorts and suntops, although sometimes we got really sunburned but didn't care. We laughed a lot and had fun with the local help.

At Christmas the farmers would give us eggs and chicken and sometimes butter which we would save and take home with us. In 1947 it snowed so much that we had to dig ourselves out of the hostel and could not get into the town for a fortnight. It was really terrible, but we all

One day while working on a mountain outside Abergavenny, a plane dropped a handful of leaflets telling us that the war was over. The pilot wrote a note asking why we were working. We looked at each other, threw our shovels down and ran to the nearest farm, who knew nothing. We had to wait until the van came to take us back to the hostel, where we put the wireless on and heard the good news. A lot of the girls were allowed home for a few days, but some had to stay to man the farms.

I wish I could live those days again. I will never forget them. I have been back to Cross Ash. Kitty Nickelson married one of the boys, and lives at Cross Ash with her three children. I can't remember all the girls' names but never will I forget my days on the land. We are all in our 70s now, but what fine, fond memories we have to tell.

Mavis Baggott,
Newport, Gwent

HARD AT WORK

TRYING TO KEEP WARM AROUND THE STOVE.

A DANCE AT THE ASSEMBLY ROOMS. WE MADE £10 FOR THE RED CROSS.

LAND GIRLS AT WORK

CHURCH PARADE AT YORK
MINSTER HELD BY THE
AGRICULTURE UNION OF
FARM WORKERS.

PULLING FLAX BY HAND.

HALLOWEEN PARTY IN THE HOSTEL - THE MEN ARE R.E.'S AND YOUNG FARMERS MEMBERS.

THE END OF A WORKING DAY.

THE END
OF A SUGAR BEET
PULLING DAY.

LIFE IN THE DORMITORY.

LADY BINGLEY GIVES A PEP TALK

LAND GIRLS AT WORK

I was in the Land Army and stationed down in Totnes, Torquay, for three years. I was called up at aged nineteen. I really wanted to go in the forces, but they wouldn't take me because then I had a very bad stammer. I had a choice between the NAAFI canteen, a factory up North or the Land Army. I chose the Land Army and was sent to a very beautiful mansion house which stood in its own grounds. The house belonged to Singer Sewing Machines, who had loaned it out to the Army. There were eighty of us Land Girls living there, with a warden in charge of us, all young girls out to have a bit of fun. The warden certainly had her hands full. We were in bed by ten o'clock with the lights out, and no talking allowed. The warden would come round to each room, which held ten girls in ten bunk beds, shine her torch on us all to make sure we were all settled down for the night, and woe betide anyone who wasn't. We were allowed one late pass a week which was on a Saturday night until twelve o'clock.

One week we were sent to a bacon factory in Totnes to make salt balls for the smokey bacon. We worked from eight to five-thirty sitting on a wooden box bagging up these little salt bags. If you had a cut on your hand the salt stung like mad. We also saw the pigs go in one end of a machine and end up in sections at the other.

Another job was painting the barges down at the docks ready for D-Day. We got more paint on us than the boats. Still on the docks, we had to pull long nails out of piles of old planks, which took all day. It was a very boring, hard job but we had some fun with the dockers. They loved us being there.

We also did a few shifts in the Cider Factory which was very old, and like working in a pit. The rotten apples they used for the cider was enough to put you off for life.

Our wage was twenty one shillings a week, ten shillings of which I sent home to my Mum. She was a widow and found it hard to live.

I remember sending my Mum a rabbit by post. I packed it in a cardboard shoe box, and nobody told me that I had to take its insides out first. The weather was very hot at the time, and as we cut the corn, rabbits were running everywhere. Unbeknown to me, my parcel got held up in the post and it took two weeks to reach Mum. The postman held it out to her at arm's length, begging her to take it, fast, as the smell was awful. With no more ado, she took it out to the back garden and buried it. I was quite cross with her, because she didn't write and thank me for what I thought had made a mouth watering rabbit pie. When it all came to light, we had a good laugh about it.

The G.I.s arrived in Totnes, about five hundred strong men. Every Saturday night the C.O. would come to the hostel with two or three lorries to take us Land Girls to their camp for the evening. Dancing was the order of the day and boy what a super Band; Joe Loss wasn't in it. The G.I.s treated us like queens. Cigs, candy, stockings were flowing like water. Many of our girls fell in love, and went back to their country to get married. My boyfriend was a Sailor whom I loved very much, but the G.I.s and I were great friends.

Every morning we girls were taken by coach and dropped at different farms to work the land in groups of two or three. My friend Jean and I were put on pulling swedes for six weeks on a very large field. After five weeks we had almost reached the end, with only a quarter left. By this time, we were sick to death of the job. One afternoon we were working alone, quite a way from the farmer and his wife, when a low flying plane passed overhead. I waved my copper at the plane as it passed, and carried on working. A few minutes later we heard the plane returning and saw it land in the corner of our field. Two men dressed in leather gear climbed out and started to walk towards us. Jean and I, being silly young things, thought that they were Germans, picked up our coppers and ran towards the farmer for help, who was working at the other end of the field. Of course they started to run too, and as they got nearer we heard them calling "Honey, wait". As the penny dropped and we realised that they were Yanks we turned and ran towards them, boy, were they handsome. They stayed with us for a couple of hours helping to pull swedes, and when it was time to go they promised they would be back the next morning at ten o'clock. They were as good as their word, and duly arrived with candy and cigs for us. They treated us with great respect and no funny

business took place. They were real gentlemen, and back at the hostel the girls were green with envy. Yes, the G.I.s were a great crowd of fellows, and when they had to move on Totnes was a very sad town. Tears were flowing in the hostel for a great number of days.

I ended my Land Army days in a punishment hostel, because I took French leave. I was there for six months, then came out on health grounds. I ended up in a factory after all, but I wouldn't have missed any of my Land Army days for the world. They were the best, and helped you to grow up and stand on your own two feet. I'm coming up to my 70th birthday soon, but I can still feel the breeches round my legs and the hob-nail boots on my feet. I miss the black high heeled court shoes we wore for best. I could not wear them now, but one can dream, can't one. What good, happy days that I often recall.

Mrs M Marvin

My friend Mabel Ridenhalgh and I were in the same W.L.A. hostel from 1943 until about 1944.

I will start right from the beginning. My friend Anne and I started going out together dancing etc, when we started working at the age of sixteen years old. At nineteen we had to register for war work. At the interviews we were told that the A.T.S. and W.A.A.Fs had got their quotas for the time being, the only things going were munitions or the Women's Land Army.

Anne and I, plus other girls loved to go over the moors hiking at weekends, so I said I would go in the W.L.A., when I told Anne she said if I was going in the W.L.A. she was coming too. We were told that friends and sisters could be together all the time. Anne and I stayed together for nearly three years and when the war ended, Anne stayed down South and I returned home to Yorkshire.

The day came to go in the W.L.A. - 26th July 1943, a Monday. We had our uniforms sent to our home. All the gear and boots, we wondered how we would get used to wearing boots. The night before the big day, I tried on all my uniform. Those baggy breeches tied at the knees. I could not bend my knees in the things, so I went upstairs to see what I looked like in them. I had to walk up the stairs like a cowboy who had been riding a horse all day; anyway we mastered the art of wearing those breeches. The green pullovers were grand too. It seems strange we were not issued with ties, we had to buy our own, also buy our own belts. In the uniform issue we had some short sleeved sports type shirts, they were a miserable fawn colour, some Land Girls decided to bleach her shirts and they bleached a lovely pale lemon shade, so we all did the same. My friend Mabel had a pair of her breeches dyed brown, they looked quite smart. Some Land Girls wore their hats on the back of their heads, and some wore them how they should have been worn - on the side of the head tilted slightly forward. There were not any regulation rules on how to wear the hat.

After six months in a W.L.A. hostel the notice board had a request for girls to do courses, four of us went on a thatching course, then months later we went on a course for milking cows. We stayed in railway carriages which were grand, really cosy, loads of hot water, bathroom and bunk beds. Wash a shirt, and half an hour later it was bone dry. There was a stone built extension on the railway carriage also.

After a fortnight we went back to the hostel. Our names then went forward for if we wanted to work on a private farm. When we were in the hostel we were taken every day to gather the harvest on different farms. I can honestly say we never had any dirty hard work to do, it was all putting wheat sheafs in stooks, and trimming overgrown hedges.

Then came threshing, a lovely job, but so very dirty and dusty. After six months my friend Anne and I got a call to say a gentleman farmer would come to see us, take us to see the farm, and if we liked it we could work for him. We liked what we saw, so we packed our bags, left the hostel, and spent the next 18 months or so ideally happy in our work. Our boss was a middle aged bachelor, he had a housekeeper and her husband worked with us on the farm.

Altogether there were six men and us two Land Girls. We only used to get one half day off a week, we only worked on the milking on a Saturday and Sunday. When the cows stayed indoors in the winter we would keep their hides clean by using a kerry comb to get the dried dung off their rear ends, and then trim their tails. One day I had been kerry combing a cow, I was bent down cleaning her legs, at the same time holding her tail down, when I straightened up and let go of her tail, what happened, without warning I got the full contents of her bowels right in the centre of my chest. I just stood and let the steaming hot dung slither off my overalls, when my boss saw me I must have looked quite a sight, it gave him a real good laugh. One day one of my cows that I was milking decided to turn round and have a good look at me. There I was, sat on my three legged stool, milk pail resting between my feet, when she came right up to my face and gave me one big lick. The lick felt so rough and powerful that I swayed on my stool, she then turned round and went on eating her nut. I reckon that was a lick of appreciation, because I used to sing to my cows. At milking time all six of us

workers milked about six or seven cows each.

With public transport few and far between we did a lot of walking from the local railway station. We applied to the W.L.A. to see if we could have the hire of a bicycle each for as long as we needed one, but they said we didn't live too far away and were not isolated enough, therefore we couldn't have a bike. Our boss being the gentleman that he was bought us one each. We had been to a famous High Street store to enquire about bikes, but as we were under twenty-one we had to have a senior person to sign for us. When we told our boss he asked if we had seen the bikes we wanted. He paid for both bikes and we paid him back at 10 shillings (50p) each until they were paid for. The cycles only cost ten pounds brand new. Very plain, black, back pedalling and brakes. We loved going for rides around the countryside in summer after work.

When Anne and I lived on the farm the housekeeper was a good cook, she was middle-aged and we had some lovely meals. We were never overworked on the far, we had a good boss and we knew we were in clover. We were very happy and contented, and felt very lucky to have been employed where we were. When I read about Land Girls having bad food and terribly hard work, I sometimes wonder if some of the farmers wives were jealous that all these attractive Land Girls had arrived in the countryside; maybe they thought their men might go astray with them.

S Middleton
Bradford, West Yorkshire.

Women's Land Army

Wearing my badge when in town
People look with a frown
What was the W.L.A? young ones ask
Working on the land was their daily task
Tractor driving, mucking out, milking too
Harvesting, potato picking they did do
They came from all walks of life
To help the War effort in its strife
Working long hours in fields on farms
Doing everything, they had no qualms
Summer threshing, baling, pitching
Choking with dust and itching
Brown as berries, we did sweat
The farmers worked us hard, you bet
Some were good to us girls on the job
Others made sure we earned our bob.
They were surprised at our skills
But didn't give us much praise.
We only helped to pay the bills.

We were happy in our work
Sometimes we grumbled but didn't shirk
In our free time, spruced and smart,
We enjoyed ourselves, but in our heart
We were proud doing our part
To help the War effort from the start
The men were fighting for our freedom
For families and the Kingdom
Women and girls took their place
War brought difficulties we had to face
Working the land, munitions, women in armed forces
Working together to pool our resources
We were glad to do our bit
So think of all the stamina and grit
As years go by we don't forget
We land girls did what we wanted to do
Helping to grow food for all of you.
So now you know what W.L.A. stood for
In years gone by when we were at war.

M J Ridehalgh

*M*ost W.L.A. girls had never had any experience on the land before and training was at a minimum, recalls Mrs G Thomson of Victoria, Australia.

'I was with the Hertfordshire War Agricultural Committee and, after very initial training, was posted to Wyddial Hall, a huge mansion near Buntingford. From there, we went out to various farms in the area doing varied jobs. Later, I was posted to Watford and the Golf Club house was made into a residential hostel for the W.L.A. The railway had evacuated their staff from London to Watford and the W.L.A. worked their market gardens to provide food for their canteens. A lot of Yorkshire girls were with the W.L.A. in Watford, and that was the first time I had ever come across the different manner of speech with the use of 'thee' and 'thou'.

Yes, it was a hard life in the fields for seven days a week, working 8 am - 5 pm and in harvest time often working until dusk.' 'There were no favours because you were a girl - I had to milk the cows at bedtime if they were newly calved' remembers Mrs Mary Temple of Flamborough, Bridlington. 'No matter how tired you were, you still had to be in the cowshed at 6 o'clock the next morning. I also remember going into the N.A.A.F.I. canteen and being told we would not be served as we were not classed as members of the Forces. My friend and I were so insulted, we never went

again, but I had some happy times in the Land Army and I still use my W.L.A. wallet that I was given when I came out after doing five years of hard slogging.'

'I think that the W.L.A. was short changed when it came to war credit. I was billeted in Eye, Suffolk, and Oh, the hard work' says Vicky Dinaro (nee Blackmore). 'We harvested from sun up to sun down, and had no recognition of ever being of help to our country'.

Mrs Knott of Dearborn, U.S.A., stayed in the W.L.A. until 1946. After changing jobs a few times while in the Land Army, she finally ended up at Woolley Rectory, Huntingdon, with nineteen other girls. Mrs. Knott went on to say 'We had no electricity or running water. It was pretty grim, but when you were young, things didn't seem to matter. The farm I was on had no men, and our boss had been a sculptress in Chelsea. As I look back I can say with all honesty that they were the happiest years of my life.

'My four years were spent on a large estate in Dorset with a G.I. camp in its park. Their rather free talk led to a leak of dates regarding the French landing. Their punishment was three weeks confined to camp. This brought General Eisenhower down for a straight talk, and I shall always remember his visit. His lady driver almost ran over me, and I ended up with the bike on top and me underneath. All I had from him was a smile and a wave. The shortage of English beer was really a punishment to the G.Is and, being a true Brit, I felt rather sorry for them and so passed bottles over the fence at night in exchange for candy and spam.' Fond memories from Mrs. J. A. James, Guernsey.

'I was billeted to a village family and allocated to a threshing machine owner, who went out to different farms except when it was very wet or windy' wrote Mrs M Robinson of Scarborough. 'Threshing was hard and extremely dirty work, and I worked with another girl managing the machine but we found that the farmers south of Bridlington would not employ us - 'It's no work for lasses' - so that was that. Shortly, we were moved to a friendly village north of Bridlington and fitted in very well. There were dances on Friday nights in the village hall to Victor Sylvester records, and I remember the amount of eggs and chips and beetroot sandwiches we got through. We sang as we cycled to and from farms in the area, and proficiency tests were organised and badges awarded. Felt triangles for each year's service were sent to us, which were sewn onto our armbands. I was in for four winters and three summers, so did not qualify for the fourth triangle'.

Mrs J Rose wrote 'I worked with three girls from Norfolk during my six years in the W.L.A. We were in Evesham, Worcestershire, and got on very well together. Our boss was the first to use gas for spraying the sprouts. The heavy shutts were about fifty yards square and were pulled by a tractor.

Four girls had to walk behind to keep it straight. All this in the heat of the day with the temperature in the 70s, and wearing gas masks. After a week, we went on strike (our wage was only 38 shillings a week). The farmer put the men on the job, who only did it for half a day and then packed it in. On offering us an extra ten shillings to do the job we said yes, because we really needed the money'.

Mrs D. J. Phiscox of Herts was stationed in a country mansion in Northamptonshire with fifty other girls. Fondly she remembers 'We had some good times, in spite of the hard work, especially harvesting and haymaking. I still laugh at one episode when twenty of us were waiting on the main road to Northampton for a lift into town. Eventually, an open backed truck stopped and the driver said that if we didn't mind climbing in the back, he would take the lot of us. We said we didn't mind, although we were wearing our best gear, so tried not to touch the sides. He took us to the town centre, as promised, then tipped the back of the truck up, rolling us all into the road. After the initial annoyance of dusting ourselves down, we had a really good laugh about it, along with all the spectators in the market square who thought it was hilarious.'

I did six and a half years in the Land Army' says Mrs W Sturges of Newbury, Berkshire, 'and my first job was looking after pigs at ICI, Bracknell. There were dozens in covered sheds and lots more in the fields. I would climb the gate, struggling with the bucket, put the feed in the troughs, then run back scared to death. Moving on to Newbury between Membury and Greeham, my new job was to take milk round the village in a van. I would dish the milk out with a ladle into jugs. I had a wonderful time. The customers gave me lots of cake and biscuits, so that by the time I had finished the round I didn't want any dinner. The Yanks were stationed close by and would whizz around the country lanes in their jeeps and fly overhead in their Monoplanes, scaring the cows and horses. They would drop in quite often to buy eggs and butter and were always courteous.'

Mrs Sheward of Dunstable, Bedfordshire, was newly married and had to register for war work and so joined the W.L.A. after her husband was reported missing. 'I wanted to drive a tractor' Mrs Sheward went on to say 'but not many of the farmers had these, owing to the shortage of petrol. I was trained for four weeks then sent to Lady Fletcher's estate where only the head gardener was left. All the others had been called up, and after a couple of months so was he. I just spent my time clearing up, and shortly Lady Fletcher sold the Hall and it was bought by the Red Cross, so I went to work for the doctor in the same village. The doctor had a pony which I thought would be a Shetland size - I was quite taken aback by the size of it. If he threw his head back, I couldn't get the halter on, and when I did he was off down the garden leaping over cabbages, etc., with me hanging on for dear life! Another of his tricks was tossing his bucket of water in the air if he didn't want it, which usually

went all over me. The chickens would get out and go under the low fir trees and I spent a long time chasing them, I have many a laugh thinking about it all'.

Mrs W Daines was stationed at Braintree during the war 'and what a life we had. The memories will stay with me for ever'. She goes on to say 'What tales we had to tell about the G.Is, especially when they mistook a band of us for prisoners of war. I soon put them right. 'Look', I said 'It's easy to tell us from them - we are the hard working, underpaid Land Girls. The prisoners travel on nice heated coaches, they have mobile canteens with nice hot meals, but we have go to make do with dried up sandwich toasted on a pitchfork in front of our fire while hedging. That's if we are able to get the fire going!' Also, the least said about our cold, damp lorries the better, which was our means of transport in those days. They were used for carting sugar beet, then hosed out ready to pick the Land Girls up. Often the floor of the lorry would be frozen in parts'.

Mrs Margaret Nelson of Bingley, West Yorkshire, served from January 1940 to December 1944, starting on a farm at Harrogate delivering milk. 'The cartons had to be made up before I could set out on the round at 7.00 am. I delivered in a Morris 12 car until petrol became very scarce, then went on to use a pony and trap. The pony became very expert on the milk round, knowing exactly where to go. Just occasionally, a colleague would do the round and when I took over again I found the pony would stop outside Marks and Spencers every morning. When I enquired why, my colleague said that she called in every morning for a coffee. The Land Girls had to work very hard but we played hard too, and had very enjoyable times. We were certainly in great demand from the Army to attend dances, and usually a three ton wagon was sent for us. I have always felt that we should have received a medal and not just an armband'.

Redenham House at Andover and Chute Stunden are well remembered by Doreen Scorey who joined the W.L.A. from Portsmouth. Her Land Girl friends nicknamed her 'Dormouse' because she always wanted to sleep,. One of her best memories is the 'after lunch fag' whilst sitting in the fields. 'It was like 'passing the parcel' as whoever had THE FAG would take the first puff, then pass it on to the next girl. It would go round the circle until it was so small that we would put it on a pin so that we wouldn't burn our fingers. Burn our lips we did, because we would not give in, knowing we might not get another puff until we saw the fellows in the evening.

Another fond memory is looking around for ladders to conveniently leave handy for the evening, when it could be put up against a nice warm hayrick for a cuddle with the latest beau. 'Often a little mouse would creep up our trouser leg, sending us into fits of laughter and a scramble down the ladder in case we were caught'.

Mrs Scorey recalls that Redenham House was very elegant, with a very smart warden called Mrs Drake-Brockman who would glide down the front stairs from her quarters, but woe betide any Land Girl who tried to use the front stairs. Theirs was the back, along with the back door. But unbeknown to Mrs Drake-Brockman, in their turn each girl had a go at sliding down that very beautiful bannister. 'In the fields were wore turbans to cover our rollers' Mrs Scorey fondly remembers. 'We went dancing to several barracks or down to the local pub where they had a set of drums. The Paras would come in for a sing-song, and of course bought us a drink because we were always broke. If you could manage to get some fags for work the next day you would be the flavour of the month. What wonderful days they were'.

Edna Keenan was one of twenty two girls who left Nottingham on 29th June 1942 to travel to Beaulieu in the New Forest. After receiving only two days tuition hoeing and singling mangolds, the girls were sent out to various farms to do all kinds of jobs. Mrs Keenan told me that the food was very poor and the girls received Forty eight shillings for a forty eight hour week. Twenty two shillings and sixpence was paid out of this for board, which later went up to twenty five shilling. Mrs Keenan goes on to say 'After eight weeks, my friend and I decided to move to a private farm but we only stayed a fortnight as it was very isolated. We made our own porridge for breakfast, and every day for a whole week we had half a pigeon each for dinner. Moving to a large farm near

Andover, I was very happy and often worked until 9.30 pm to get the work done in the good weather. It was hard work but I enjoyed it, and found the energy to go dancing in the evening - all this after lifting sacks of potatoes on my back!

We also had our frightening moments too. My friend and I were coming from the village pub one night when a Buzzbomb came overhead. The engine suddenly stopped and we threw ourselves down in the ditch. Seconds later, it exploded two fields away.

One day, whilst in the process of littering a large area with straw for the heifers, I jabbed my two pronged fork into a bale with some force, missed, and went through two pairs of socks, trousers, and wellington boots into my leg. The others laughed until they realised how badly it hurt. After a very painful, sleepless night I found my leg three times its normal size and the Doctor was sent for. He gave me a tetanus injection and I remember that two weeks later, in a borrowed slipper two sizes too large, I had to cycle in the best way that I could the seven miles to see him. Four years later I had a small operation to remove a tiny round piece of rubber (from my wellington) from my ankle. It had moved three inches in those years, and the Doctor said how lucky I was that it had not gone further upwards.

A lady who did not wish to give her name wrote 'With the coming of the 1939/45 war came changes and I was one of many - when the words release, excitement and a whole new way of life came into being, it was difficult to imagine. My choice was the W.R.E.Ns but my parents found the correspondence and I was immediately sent away to live in the country (imagine, at the age of twenty and three quarters). It was in this country retreat that I met two Land Army girls working the estate, and with great care I too joined the W.L.A. From that day, my parents never spoke to me or had any contact with me again.

As a W.L.A. member I started a new way of life - even now, it's difficult to describe the sense of freedom which helped to take care of the tiredness with all the very different ways of life, and a work start of 6.00 am which went on until evening. As I became more skilled, I moved to a fairly large Cheshire farm still run on the old traditional ways, with horses, cows milked by hand, and not a mechanical thing in sight. We got water from a well or pump. What an experience; so much so that when the war ended, I stayed on that farm for a further six years until by scraping and saving all the time, I obtained the tenancy of a very small farm.

Working very hard, harder that I ever thought possible, I prospered. I had no time for a husband and followed what was still considered a sensible way of life for a woman. As time went by, I moved to a farm of my own and my pleasure is today to lean on a field gate looking at animals which I won, and consider that as a result of the war and my Land Army training, my life is full of interest. Not as young as I was, I still work a full farming day on a small farm I have away in the hills. The Land Army gave me an escape route to a life of happiness, a love of the countryside and, above all, contentment.'

Gwyneth Nesbitt joined the W.L.A. in 1943 and worked in the Pest Department. To use her own words, 'Catching rats in the most depressing places was not the most enjoyable of jobs, but I lived in a Manor House in Clwyd, then called Flintshire, a wonderful place to live. Soon I was taught to drive and moved on to Queensbridge to a hostel in Overton where I stayed for a few months. Meanwhile, I was a driver picking up from various hostels besides working on the land. During this time I met my G.I. husband who travelled between London and Tidworth, escorting war brides.
Shortly afterwards I was a G.I. bride too, and sailed for America.'

Mrs Mary Wedge Craig of Pangbourne, Berkshire, writes 'I joined the W.L.A. in December 1941 with my friend Pat Cooper. We were both aged 19, and had been insurance clerks since leaving school.

We were called up in February 1942 and sent to Rodbaston Hall, Penkridge, Staffordshire, for four weeks' basic training, as follows:-

1 week Pigs
1 week Poultry
1 week Dairy
1 week General Farming.

Donald Carpenter was the Assistant Bailiff on whom several of us had an enormous crush: at least it helped get over the homesickness.

Pat Cooper and I were sent to separate farms in Wiltshire. I had digs in a small cottage - the family had to go through my bedroom to reach the stairs. We had an outside loo and no electricity. The farm was primitive - the cows were not combed or washed before hand milking and the dirt from one's hands dripped into the milk. The sheds were never washed and the dung was just shovelled out and brushed into a heap in the yard. Stones, etc., were mixed with the dung which was then spread on the fields. After milking, my first job was stone picking - walking up and down the fields with a bucket picking up the stones so that they wouldn't break the cutting blades during haymaking. I was homesick and walked up and down by myself crying all the while. The hand milking caused my hands to swell and my arms ached so much that I could not sleep. In the end, I couldn't close my hands round the cows' teats so Doctor suggested that I was transferred to a farm with a milking machine.

Pat Cooper and I then went to a farm near Lyneham airbase. Planes were dispersed around our fields, and we shared a double bed in a room with a Priest hole in the cupboard - I didn't see the family ghost but he did open our door and then the cupboard door and presumably went down the Priest hole, which was connected to the local Church. We were fired after four months because the cowman's son followed Pat Cooper around all day instead of getting on with his work. The farmer said he could get other Land Girls - he could not replace the boy.

Our next job was at Petersfinger, near Salisbury; a mixed farm with about 40 cows in milk. A home farm, water meadows and staff including Dairyman Carter and a man on piece work hoeing, etc. The farmer did occasional tractor driving on the arable farm of about 100 acres at Whiteparish. One man was in charge with part time help from his young son. I used to drive the tractor with harrow cultivator, etc. We were originally in Digs but the Landlady decided my face did not fit, so I was moved into the farm. The Landlady died some time later so Pat Cooper then joined me at the Farm.

I married a Naval Officer in May 1943 and left the Land Army in 1944 because he had found a Flat near his base - sadly this was cancelled, because all Ports were closed before D Day so I returned to my parents in London.'

Mary finally sums up her Land Army days as follows:-

Plusses: Being in the country, being well fed at the last job, and a nice family.

Minuses: One week's paid leave a year - half a day a week which we worked, and took a sort weekend leave once a month. Uniform had to be returned on leaving, and we got 12 clothing coupons with which to start civilian life. Lack of medical supervision - no tetanus injections were ever given. The heavy work created spinal damage, which has troubled me ever since.

'*I* spent four years in the W.L.A. from 1942 to 1946. Thirty of us occupied a block at the R.A.F. Hostel in Hereford. We had the advantage of good E.N.S.A. and C.E.M.A. shows, and also dances. Later it became a good behaviour billet; if we disobeyed the rules, we were sent to outlying hostels.

Each morning we went out by van on a ten mile radius. We were the first Land Girls in the country and not popular with the farmers. I started in July with fruit picking - blackcurrants, loganberries, and on to plums and apples. The farm was attached to a manor house and the fruit plantation was large. We worked with fruit pickers from over the Welsh border, who resented our presence. In October we went potato picking at Gredenhill where there was an R.A.F. camp. Locals, knowing we were new to the job, moved our stakes and we were always scrambling to finish the row before the tractor came along. A student staying on the farm moved them back and came to work with us.

We pulled beet in severe frosty weather when we were so cold and hungry that we ate our lunch sandwiches in the morning break. After a very wet spell we were sent home for four days while the War Ag. provided the necessary gum boots. The local doctor refused to treat any more colds until they did so.

There were a lot of armed forces in Hereford. We joined a church club where we played table tennis and darts, where the church ladies provided refreshments and also stationery to write letters home. The G.I.s were more in evidence in the pubs and at hostel dances, although a very good American choir once gave a concert at the church. We chatted with a pleasant coloured boy who said that his name was James Mason, and that he found it very embarrassing at times.

I was a quiet, serious girl with a hearing problem; not the type to attract boys much. One of our nicer girls was friendly with an American soldier who liked to walk along the river and quote poetry to her. I travelled home as far as Crewe with her, and she confided that she was fond of him, but wasn't sure of his intentions. Later she received a parcel from his Mother in America, and she eventually married him.

We did the usual work on the land - threshing, planting potatoes, hoeing, weeding the young corn, tying hops, haymaking and harvesting, sewing sacks on wet days, or white washing farm buildings. My friend and I usually worked on a farm within walking distance on the bank of the river, but we were moved in the busy season for more important jobs. It was at another farm which was also within walking distance that we came in contact with G.I.s. We were threshing at the farm of a retired Colonel who owned a lot of land in the county - a bailiff looked after the one where we were working. He lived in one of a row of cottages which, with a convent, and a convent school taken over by the Americans, was the entire village. The wife of the bailiff who usually brewed our tea was away for the day, there was no answer from the other cottages, so our bravest girl knocked on the side door of the school. The soldier who answered was horrified at our request for tea, but we were all invited in for coffee. Quite a crowd gathered in the canteen, and when they found that we only had cheese sandwiches to eat, one went and came back with four steaming plates on a tray - meat and diced vegetables. This was followed by fruit salad and ice-cream, all remains from the officer's mess and destined for the pig bin. When we left they promised to come and help, and two of them did. The bailiff sent them on to the hay and they pitched all after noon until we had finished. They dated two of the girls. It was our last day on the farm, at only one farm were we ever provided with a hot meal, and here the entire staff sat down together.

We worked hard, sometimes late into the evening when haymaking or harvesting, but on the whole it was a happy time. Joys and sorrows were shared. Some of the boys we had played tennis with were killed, some boyfriends came home, some girls married boys they met in Hereford, three married G.I.s, one a Canadian. As there was less need of us we went home, some to get married, some to be united with husbands and boyfriends. My own romance wasn't a success, and my Father died.

I found the G.I.s that I met very generous but rather larger than life.'

Dorothy Hodkinson

'**I** am an ex W.L.A. girl. I joined in 1943 aged seventeen and a half years old.

We were billeted in Dorchester in Bridport, Dorset - teaming with G.Is.
We were on pest destruction, earning a little more than other W.L.A. girls. It was considered a nasty job. (I think we earned 25 shillings and gave our landlady 12/- 6d for our board.)

We trapped and poisoned rats mostly, but occasionally we gassed foxes and badgers. We went out each morning with an ex-farmer and his dogs in a battered old Austin. One morning we somehow or other found ourselves in the middle of an American convoy and amid shouts and curses, we held them up whilst we were allowed to extricate our car. G.Is were leaping from the backs of huge trucks, trying to chat us up (two giddy blondes) and yelling 'timber' at our boss (the ex-farmer).

Thumbing a lift from Dorchester, returning to our billet, being picked up by a V.S. Sergeant in jeep, and then realising an American Lieutenant was sitting in the back, and his mild comment, 'We are not allowed to haul women around in a government vehicle Sergeant.' This remark was completely disregarded and conversation on other matters took place.

Thumbing a lift to London on a Bank Holiday weekend and being picked up by a Red Cross ambulance (American) I asked the driver if he had any patients in the back and was informed yes, and they had the 'clap'. I was so innocent I did not know the meaning of this, until he explained!

We often found it difficult to have a bath as our billet was very primitive and was advised by another W.L.A. member to go to a lady in the town (Bridport) who allowed forces people to take a hot bath. The only payment was to be a 2¹/₂d stamp (so she could correspond with overseas troops). It was snowing and I went along to find the house teeming with G.I's hanging out of upstairs windows, with kettles in thier hands, trying to unfreeze pipes which were frozen. This lady was quite eccentric and had a very large house with several floors, and she entertained many, many G.Is. It was hilarious, the commotion and confusion, with boys up and down stairs with kettles.

We played table tennis each evening in the Y.M.C.A. with the boys, and had quite a lot of fun. We took them back occasionally and introduced them to our landlady who was then showered with cans of peaches, flashlights and various gifts - at a later date.

The black G.Is did not mix with the white and we only saw them in church on Sundays singing in the choir. Our landlady brought several of them home one evening. It was quite innocent because her Mother and Father came along also. The black boys were learning to play 'shove halfpenny' with this lady's Father.

That evening I went along to meet my boyfriend (the V.S. Sergeant) and he was furious. He had seen the black boys go into the house and thought we had invited them! That was the first time I encountered hatred of blacks. If a black soldier asked for directions and you answered his request you were told (by the whites) in no uncertain terms to ignore them. This happened to me (an American military policeman actually left the traffic he was directing, in the middle of the road to admonish me!)

The convoys were on each side of the road, prior to the invasion and it was very sad after they all pulled out. I missed their friendly faces; they taught me so much. The courtesy, their politeness and their camaraderie with their officers.

We once again broke down in heavy traffic and the fault was mine!

Each day we took our lunch in village pubs or if the weather was fine ate our sandwiches in the fields where we were working. (We were laying gin traps or collecting them and wringing the necks of those poor rabbits.) In retrospect I think it was so cruel!

Often a couple of tents were erected in these fields containing a handful of American troops with various instruments. They showed great interest in our work and followed us around asking questions. They usually offered us coffee around lunch time.

This day, we were alone in the field and my boss suggested making tea. This I was loathe to do because of lighting a fire. He usually made the tea but asked me to perform this task. My efforts were once again unsuccessful - I could not get the fire started. I told him so and he suggested I take on old sock from the back of the car (he kept a collection of rags, clothes and old socks in the back of the car with his dogs.) He then advised me to insert a long stick into the sock and dip it into the petrol tank. Once soaked in petrol and placed on the fire, the first would start with ease. Unfortunately, several socks failed to emerge, but I eventually got the fire going with the fourth sock - which did emerge.

I haven't really described our job on pest destruction - we girls doing this job were very few and far between. We called in at farms and barns and the farm people would tell us of the infestation. We laid a certain poison around farms - this was harmless to farm animals and pets, but lethal to rats. This poison caused agony in rats and they took 48 hours to die. We collected the dead and buried them on Saturday mornings. 1944 - Thousands more troops arrived from the U.S. and were ensconced in the woods opposite our billet. This camp was called D2 which Eisenhower visited. We frequently visited the boys in their nissen huts and tents, enjoying their coffee and food. We rode in their tanks and had a jolly good time. When they went off to Devon on manoeuvres for about a week we were

asked to take care of their money which was won in 'crap' games. This consisted of hundreds and hundreds of pound. (They did not wish to leave this money in camp.) We casually took this to our billets and put in the chest of drawers. The landlady became very suspicious and wrote to my Mother (despite my explanation) because she did not believe my story.

If you have every watched Sergeant Bilko on television, you will have some idea of the amount of money that changed hands in these 'crap' games. The noise and shouting as they threw the dice was unbelievable!'

Marion Gilbert
Forest Hill, London.

Spring

I have seen such lovely things -
A butterfly with golden wings.
A blackthorn's snow against a sky,
That's surely borrowed from July

And fields of barley newly rolled,
In strips of jade and emerald.
The sheen of dew upon the grass,
And wild flowers nodding as you pass.

The brown and yellow bumble bee,
The gleam of sunshine on the sea.
All these I've seen, such lovely things,
On sunny days when April sings.

D M Strange 26538

Sussex

'**F**or too long our contribution to the last war effort has been largely ignored.

I served from June 1941 until I was demobbed in October 1945. After working on small farms (near Heathrow) and a remote farm at Tolleshunt Knights near Tiptree in Essex, I finally ended up at Stansted in a specially built hostel for thirty girls. Our work was carried out in the surrounding area on small farms. However, in late 1941 rumours were that the Yanks were coming to our area. They finally arrived about March 1942. The quiet little village of Stansted was turned upside down, but our job was to clear all the produce for miles around so that runways could be put down, so we girls quite literally helped to build Stansted Airport. We pulled beet and potatoes, etc, stacked wheat, while the bulldozers followed us putting down concrete.

Our social life altered somewhat. Our lives were turned into glamorous evenings at the local pub drinking ginger wine and watered down beer, and eating onion and carrot sandwiches. Among the Yanks were smart New Yorkers, callow youths from Louisiana, hill-billies, etc. They came and went in the space of eighteen months, leaving behind many broken hearts. The Yanks we met were a most generous, happy-go-lucky bunch of men. Of course in 1942, when they first arrived, most of us were already war-weary. Many of us were Londoners who had been bombed and blitzed and, in my case, machine-gunned by a lone

Messerschmitt whilst walking down the street! So when these gorgeous and glamorous creatures descended on our little village during the night, our whole world turned upside down. Their smart uniforms, their exuberance and happy laughter during such a grim time in the War acted like a tonic to us all.

I organised Saturday night dances in our hostel. They were quite a hit with both the English and American soldiers stationed nearby, although I must confess the harmony was a little less when they all got together.

There were some rather funny incidents. Although our Supervisor would not allow any liquid refreshments, some of the boys did used to smuggle in some beer. One, Freddie Bamberger did rather over-do the imbibing. We girls were in the ablution block after the festivities, when a loud snore was heard. It came from a locked toilet. On looking over the top, we saw Freddie fast asleep. In our dressing gowns we rushed out into the road, and managed to stop a passing M.P. jeep. They managed to smuggle him out without our Supervisor hearing a thing, because if she had, it would have meant the end of our dances.

Some of us used to go to the American Red Cross Canteen to serve coffee and doughnuts, etc, and generally to be friendly with the boys. Many a romance started there. It had a wonderful atmosphere after the drudgery of picking sugar beets and stacking heavy bales of wheat. I even took my sister up there on several occasions. She

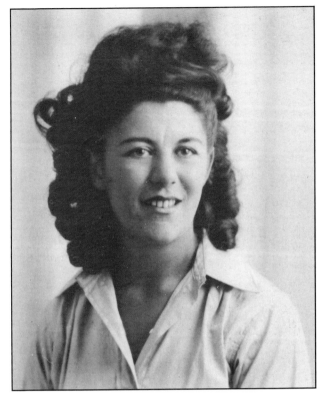

ON LEAVE 1944

was serving her War in the Tank Corps - repairing tanks! She had never seen the Yanks before, and was rather overwhelmed. At the time, when one came over and asked her for a Coke, she was a little puzzled and came over and asked me where she could get a piece of coke from. No kidding! I had to explain to her that what he wanted was a Coca-Cola (which we hadn't seen in this country before) and not a piece of combustible fuel! As the camp was situated near the large airfield in Cambridge, many German Bombers would fly

ANN BERNSTEIN
FIRST WEEK IN THE LAND ARMY HOUNSLOW 1941

over our hostel to get to the airfield. Consequently, we became known as Flying Bomb Alley. Many a time we had to dive under the table and chairs when the alarm went off.

Then came D.Day! - June 6th. We knew something was up when we heard dozens of trucks driving past our hostel late at night. The next morning, dozens of bombers, with the yellow markers, flew overhead. We all knew then that the beginning of the end was in sight.

Meanwhile, we worked in sparse conditions. For instance, we were sent out on icy cold days with a couple of sandwiches of beetroot or shredded carrots. It was only due to the kindness of the Yank cooks that we had some decent food. They would send beef sandwiches over, other goodies and cigarettes because they felt so sorry for us. Of course they thought we were pretty wonderful too!

I have very special memories of V.E. Day. We had a celebration at the American Red Cross, but a lot of the G.Is were not too happy as they knew that it meant their being posted to the Pacific war zone, which is exactly what happened. I met my sister in London and we were crammed together with thousands in Trafalgar Squire. It was quite frightening - we got swept away from each other. People just went mad. I was pleased to get back to the relative calm at Stansted 'village'.

Ann Bernstein
London

HEDGING AND DITCHING AT RENFREW FARM WITH THE HELP OF THE 8th ARMY (US) - STANSTED 1944

ANN BERNSTEIN, SECOND FROM LEFT - STANSTED 1944.

PHOTO BY BY L.T. HANK HANNA US ARMY.

LAND GIRLS AT WORK

'I joined the W.L.A. in 1945 when I was 17. After reporting at the main office at Aylesbury, I got one month's basic training for all the jobs on the farm, along with my friend who had joined up at the same time as me.

We were sent to a hostel at Terrick Cross, near Chequers. There were about twenty girls, and we would be picked up every morning by lorry and taken to different farms where help was needed. Potato picking, ditching, singling, or any other outdoor job we did. My friend Eve and I went into a Threshing Team and were sent all over Bucks in the summer, harvesting, stooking, or cutting thistles down.

After two years on field work, Eve and I volunteered for milking and tractor driving. We did a month's training and then we were S.O.S., which meant we were sent to different private farms. That's when Eve and I lost touch. I ended up at Firgest near Henley on Thames, and worked at a farm near a village called Hambleden.

While billeted at the hostel at Firgest, I worked a farm at Dorton Wooten, Underwood. A Major owned all the estate and I had to stay at the farm bailiff's house. I used to get myself up at 6.30 am, and go down to the shed where the cows were laid in winter. It was freezing cold, and by the light of an oil lamp I had to wash the cows' udders in cold water, then milk them with the help of an old man of eighty. He used to give me a drink of black tea, out of an even blacker flask, but it used to taste like nectar to me. I went to the farmhouse for breakfast, but all I got was lumps of cold, fat bacon. I never had an egg all the time I was in the W.L.A. I worked on this farm for months and never finished until six at night. Fat bacon was all I ever saw of food, and if I hadn't drank some of the milk, I wouldn't have survived.

I went out with the tractor and trailer, cutting kale and taking it to feed the cattle, which was hard work. When I put down the hours I worked which included weekends - Saturdays and Sundays with no let up - the Bailiff would say "The Major won't like paying for all these hours. You don't need to put them all down, do you?" I think he was afraid of losing his job; there were a few farms on the estate owned by the Major.

I put in for two weeks' leave, and on my return they wanted to send me to the same farm. I told them "No way will I go back there", so I was sent back to the hostel which was now at Berryfield, and on to the private farm again, which I really liked.

In the summer, if we had a weekend off we would go to see the underground trains, which were a novelty to us, coming from Yorkshire. I lived at Manningham, Bradford.

Everything was so different for us in the Land Army. When we were in the hostels we never got good food. If you didn't get down early in the morning there wasn't anything left to make a sandwich with, and sometimes we went all day without a drink.

We worked on field working sometimes with Italian and German prisoners. The farmers used to treat them better than us. To some of the farmers we were just a joke, but they soon found out that we were as good as the men at our work. I think we used to earn about £1.5.0d., out of which we spent most of it in canteens on beans on toast.

My Mother used to knit things like gloves and socks. She also sent me clothing coupons for underwear, etc.

We used to go to the village dance on Saturday nights at Butlers Cross, Chequers. We were not supposed to know when Winston Churchill was at Chequers, but when the Guardsmen were not at the dance, we knew that Winston was in residence. On Sunday mornings we would go to the village church and see him in his pew.

Isabel Rawlings Barnett, as she was then, came to our hostel - something to do with National Savings. I always remember her, she had such lovely laughing eyes.'

Mrs Ridehalyh
Colne, Lancashire

'I was in the Women's Land Army from early 1943 to 1946, and was stationed in Cornwall, being at Pencubitt Hostel, Liskeard, for most of that time.

There were quite a few camps around Liskeard and district. I remember pre D Day; each American camp used to compete with each other to entertain us. Each Saturday night they would send a lorry to take us all to their camp. There would be a super band, where we used to show our skills at jitterbugging! Also, long tables piled high with spam sandwiches and all the things we couldn't get because of rationing. Packs of Lucky Strike cigarettes, 200 all at once! We felt like film stars.

Most Saturday nights in the summer, a crowd of us would go to Looe and meet the yanks. We had all coupled off at this stage. Then they would pay for us (5/- for B & B) to stay at Looe for bed and breakfast, and because there were not trains on Sundays back to Liskeara, they would pay for us to go back in a taxi; about 10/-, which was a fortune to us, and the Yanks would go back to camp. Can you imagine that happening today without any strings attached?! They were real good fellas - I never knew of anyone getting into 'trouble', we just had good, clean fun. How we all enjoyed ourselves. One girl called Marian had her engagement ring sent over in a box of chocolates from America. She had her wedding reception at the hostel - we all put together for the clothing coupons for her outfit. Because

MRS D PLATTS (TOP ROW THIRD FROM RIGHT) POTATO PICKING GANG 1943

D-Day was looming, her G.I. wasn't allowed far from camp, so they spent their honeymoon at the nearest farmhouse. A week later he was killed on D-Day, so that was a sad occasion. I know she went to the States after the war. I often wonder what became of her.'

Dorothy Platts
Sheffield.

GIRLS OF PENCUBITT
HOSTEL JULY 1944.

PENCUBITT HOSTEL JULY 1944

'**D**. Day - 6th June 1944 - A never to be forgotten day!

Arriving as usual at the farm, I had collected the cows from their grazing meadows and had started milking, when we heard the sound of aircraft approaching (which was quite unusual for early morning), and running out we saw quite a number of flights of fighters coming up the valley from Whitley way towards us at Grayswood. Giving them a cheer, we returned to our milking machines when about half an hour later we heard a low, groaning sound of heavy

AUDREY EASTMAN 1944

aircraft, and upon running out of the sheds again we knew that somewhere the invasion of Western Europe had begun. The whole sky seemed to be full of Dakotas towing one or two gliders. This magnificent, but frightening, pageantry of the skies continued all day, only easing a little towards nightfall. Then, thirty six hours later, the ambulance trains were arriving at Haslemere station where the wounded were, oh so carefully, transferred to one of the military ambulances which were in a line some half a mile long through the streets.

For a few days now, most of the workers on the local farms had been occupied in cutting dead wood form hedges and woods to celebrate victory in Europe, and carting it all to our village green to make a magnificent bonfire. When the evening arrived and people and troops from all the surrounding areas wended their way to the green, the fire was lit and blazed upwards, and then a Nightingale sang. It sang loud and clear, and for a few moments the whole assemblage was hushed. The bird sang on and this little miracle ended when the dying embers and the few remaining people faded into the night.

On the evening of peace, myself and a few Land Army friends found ourselves in Haslemere where there was much joyous singing and dancing in the Square. Then, as it was getting dark, army lorries arrived and were placed inwards and shone the headlights into the crowd, so that the whole Square was floodlit. That was a wonderful evening. How sad it is that it takes a war, or some other dreadful tragedy, for everyone to pull together. It was a wonderful time for us. How different our peace in England's countryside to our Force's hell in foreign lands.'

Audrey Eastman
Weybridge, Surrey

AUDREY - WINNIE - MR PERRETT - FLORRIE

WITH THE STABLE CAT

AUDREY
AND
LOVING
FRIENDS

Lonely Land Girl

May I protest in written rhyme,
Re those two girls in the gardening line.
Who, not having enough to do,
Did volunteer for overtime?
Send them to me, those volunteers,
Send them to me, complete with shears;
There's overtime enough for years
Where I am!

Send Pat and Joan and a few Rosemaries
To help me straw the good strawberries.
Send me a girl to pick the fruit;
Beside the lake, beneath the trees,
Fluttering and dancing in the breeze
Where I am!

I grow the finest crop of hay,
Was ever seen down Cheshire way.
I want a girl to mow it down,
And cart it off in someone's dray.
A volunteer who would not blench;
At something I dare scarcely mench,
(The length of a half-dug celery trench)
Where I am.

Someone to raise the fallen hop,
To fetch the mower from the shop.
To lend a hand with the spinach beet,
And thin me out the carrot crop.
Send me only a couple more,
Though I could do with half a score;
To help the Land Girl win the war
Where I am!

"Connie" W.L.A. 46587
Cheshire

Chapter 2

LAND GIRLS AND THE G.I.s

'I am Dorothy Joyce Mahanowski of West Derby, Liverpool, England. I was born in 1924 which made me seventeen years of age during that horrible time of May 1941 blitz; I was waiting to be old enough to join the W.L.A. Being a city girl my Dad tried to put me off by saying 'They'll have you up at five-thirty in the morning to milk the cows'. It never happened.

In 1942 I joined, and was sent to Hope House, Foxhall Road, Ipswich. This had been an orphanage, but the orphans had been sent to the country for safety. Sixty W.L.A. girls were housed at Hope House and I got along fine, having five sisters at home I was used to female company.

After a while I was promoted to Forewoman in charge of sixty girls, and taught to drive a Hillman Minx van. I drove the girls to various farms, they had to be there by 7.00 am each morning. If the farms were not too far away some would go by bus, and some rode bicycles. I must say here, that I really loved my three

and a half years in the W.L.A., they were some of the best years of my life.

I chose my friend, Vera Pilkington as my Ganger. She married a G.I., but sadly died after the birth of her baby. We were at Ipswich, a small town surrounded by American bases, my boyfriend Len was a G.I. and sometimes we were invited to share a meal at base. They had so much to eat - pound slabs of real butter every few feet down the table. Food was served cafeteria style and the server would slap marmalade on to your mashed potatoes whether you wanted it or not.

In February 1945 Len hitchhiked to England from Belgium, he wanted us to marry, so I got leave and we went up to Liverpool. My Dad said no to marriage; it was three weeks before my 21st Birthday and I needed permission 'till then.

On May 8th the war was over. By October, Lens outfit, 482nd Engineers were preparing to leave for the U.S.A. He'd applied for marriage approval from the Army but it hadn't arrived. It turned out they had flown it to Belgium as Len crossed to England! To cut a long story short, on the strength of a telegram we had received from the Chaplain saying, 'Marriage approval arriving U.S. embassy.' The Chief Registrar made Len swear he wasn't already married in the U.S., then gave us a licence. This was 13th October 1945, so the wedding plans went ahead. Our 2.00 pm time was no longer available so the Minister made it for 4.00 pm. Everyone had saved rations and my dear old Mum had made our wedding cake. The baker had decorated it and the Union Jack and Old Glory were crossed on the top tier.

One of my bridesmaids, my thirteen year old sister Iris, was at the hairdressers for the first time in her young life. It was time for the bridesmaids to leave for the church, but Iris wasn't home yet. I got on my Dad's bike and rode to the shop. Iris was under the dryer with her hair still wet. I dragged her out of the shop and made her sit on the crossbar of the bike, it hurt her and she was crying; then, going round a corner and downhill we fell off. My leg was bleeding and Iris cried even more. We arrived home to find Len in the back kitchen wearing my Mother's dressing gown and trying to iron his pants!! (not very romantic). As he left for church he said if I wasn't on time he wouldn't wait for me!! I couldn't find my new underwear, my petticoat had been made from a used parachute, I had a bloody leg which hurt, and no time to have a bath! Ready at last, I asked the limousine to hurry, but Dad told him to slow down so that I could wave to all the neighbours who lined the street.

Len had waited for me, I was almost hysterical by this time, and Len didn't help matters any when told by the Minister to 'repeat after me', he got to 'I plight thee my troth.' But when Len said it, it came out, 'I plight thee my throat.' Just like a circus! Len was scheduled to depart on 15th October 1945 for the continent. The following day we rode a train to Ipswich where we said goodbye, me to the W.L.A., Len to his outfit on the continent, and demob in the U.S.A.

My sister Muriel was in the A.T.S. and had asked for permission to attend my wedding, but it was not granted, she came anyway and brought a girlfriend. On their return they were picked up by Redcaps at Lime Street Station and arrested, absent without leave, and put on scrubbing floors for two weeks.

I was not to see Len again for eight months 'till June 1946 when I arrived at New York aboard the Swedish Liner 'Holbrook'. One year later I gave birth to twin boys.

It is now 46 years later and we are still together. Yes, I have a lot to thank the W.L.A. for.'

Dorothy Joyce Mahanowski
America.

'I was one of a gang of Land Girls who worked on the land during 1940 to 1946' says Vera Hoffmann. 'We were issued with breeches, greatcoats and dungarees, similar to those worn by the Land Army girls. We worked on the fields cutting turnips, swede, sugar beet, and other vegetables which were distributed to Army Camps. We travelled in an open truck all over Suffolk, coming back after a long day's work, sometimes late at night sitting on top of a load of bagged veg; singing at the tops of our voices the latest songs of that time, sometimes wet through.

When the first G.Is came to Suffolk in 1943 we were told they would be arriving by train. We were also told they were the black G.Is. As we had never seen a live black man, we went down to the station to greet them, expecting to see men in grass skirts holding spears. Instead they all alighted from the train in very smart fatigues. They were the first G.Is to arrive to lay the runways on the American Air Bases at Debach, Parham and Horham - all in Suffolk. After the runways were laid, one of our jobs was to visit the airbases to pick up stones from the runways; during one of those visits three huge bomber planes were grounded on one of the runways; they had come in for a service. A G.I. (white) said we were not allowed to talk to the black G.Is, then he let us look over one of the planes. They were very grim inside, dark and cold, very uncomfortable for the crew, I should imagine.

One of the bombers was the 'Memphis Belle'. I believe they have now made a film about the crew.

We were also invited to their dances which the G.Is had on occasions. These were held in huge hangers at different bases. Glenn Miller and his band were flown over from the States to entertain the G.Is at one of these 'do's' - it was a magical evening which I shall never forget. My sister, who was a Land Army girl billeted in a village north of Woodbridge called Syts, also came to the dance and was presented with a posy for being the best dancer (jitterbugging) that year. She married an American Marine and now lives in St Antonio, Texas'.

Mrs Gordon From London recalls 'I lived for a year in North Devon during the blitz looking after my Mother, who had to be evacuated from London. We came back to London in 1941, but I couldn't stand not being in the country. As I was due to be called up, I volunteered for the W.L.A. and was sent to Cornwall.

I thoroughly enjoyed my life, and during the winter months I was in a private billet in Truro. We worked in a gang and went potato picking, which was monotonous.

From February until September each year I worked on the same two farms in Helston, doing the normal farm work. They were lovely people on each farm, and I had it very easy; lucky not to be turning out at the crack of dawn - I was in bed until 7.00 am then up for breakfast at 8.00 am. On one farm there were two young children, and I often baby-sat so that the farmer and his wife could go to the pictures.

Men were scarce; all the locals were either in the forces or married, so it was like a breath of fresh air when the G.Is arrived. They had their camp on one of the farms where I worked, so I got to know quite a few of them.

During haymaking you would find Yanks turning up in the field to work with you; I expect they were from farms back home. With the exception of the odd couple, we found them friendly, generous and easy to get along with, and I didn't meet one that bragged about what he had back home.

On the evening of D Day it reminded me of a film scene with all the G.Is crowding round the wireless in the farmhouse listening to General Eisenhower's speech on how things were going in France.

When the G.Is pulled out and all the tents were gone, the place seemed desolate. When we went back to Truro that winter, the town was swarming with American Navy and Cost Guards that were serving on L.S.T.s (Landing Ships Tanks). They came to Truro because there were so many permanently based in Falmouth that the L.S.Ts coming back from France didn't stand a chance with the girls at the dances.

So it was dates every night - still the G.Is, but the uniform changed again. I was lucky with the types that I met at the dances - if they offered to take you home it was jut that, no fighting off amorous lads. My landlady used to plead with me not to marry a Yank, but wait for our boys to come home. I did get one proposal of marriage, but turned it down although we remained friends and I saw him off on his last leave before he left for the U.S.A.

Long ago now, but good memories that I often think of. I was glad of the opportunity to learn to love the countryside, and to know the G.Is'.

'**M**y three sisters and I were all in the Land Army. We worked at Hale Nurseries, Woodgreen, near Fordingbridge, Hampshire. We were lucky as we lived in the village. There was a Hostel at the nurseries where many W.L.A. girls lived. They came from all over the country, but we had to travel miles for any entertainment.

One evening we were cycling home from work and there were two Yanks leaning against the pub fence. They stopped us and asked if we would like to go to a dance. Of course we jumped at the chance. They asked if we knew any more girls who would like to go, so we directed them to the Hostel.

At 7.30 that evening the Yanks came back with a large truck and we all piled in. When we arrived at the dance hall there were hundreds of Yanks. We all had a wonderful time jiving and dancing. Best of all was eating hot doughnuts which were cooked on the spot. We all ate too much, after being rationed with food, and all felt a bit ill in the morning.

The G.I.s were stationed in the next village - Breamore - for about nine months, by which time most of us had an American boyfriend. Some of the girls got married and were sadly let down, as I was myself. I was engaged, and managed to get clothing coupons from everyone I knew to buy my trousseau. I borrowed a white wedding gown; by this time, my boyfriend had been posted to France. I received at least two letters a week, then suddenly my letters to him were returned to me marked "not known". I wrote to his Mother in Indiana, and although she had written many times, this time there was no answer. I don't know to this day what happened.

We mostly grew tomatoes and picked up potatoes which was pretty back-breaking. The potato fields were miles away and we travelled there in a big van. It was near an Airfield called Irsley, where American Airmen were stationed. We were invited to their dances, so there was never a dull moment.'

Lillian Taylor
London

'I joined the W.L.A. when I was twenty. I was very lucky to get in as I had a stroke when I was eighteen, but was good at hiding that I was a little weaker on the right side. As luck would have it, my interviewer came from Hampshire, as did my Mother.

I went to Norfolk to do my training and stayed in a big house with a large smelly pond outside. We were near the American air bases, and one G.I. called Lee wanted me to go for a drink with him in the next village. Our transport would be by bike, and not having one of my own, several of the G.I.s searched their camp and collected bits and pieces enough to build me one. When it was finished I wouldn't ride it because it had a crossbar, so they took it off and welded it so that I had a ladies bike. On the way back to base, one of the G.I.s fell off his bike, broke his leg and was sent back to America. I later heard that he was given the Purple Heart; I never did learn what for. Lee said that he was going to take me back to the States with him after the war but that I would have to wear contact lenses instead of glasses, so that was the end of that little affair!

Soon after I was sent to another farm whose cow shed was opposite the base hospital. The G.I.s used to lean over the door and chat. I got many a tin of fruit, chocs and bars of soap. Once I even got a pair of scissors.

I went to a village dance and had never seen so

many men at once in one place - nearly all G.I.s. I loved dancing so I had a great time. Doing a real fast turn my G.I. partner twisted me round too fast and I twirled across the floor and sat down next to a G.I. on the other side of the room. I lost one partner and gained another.

One day I was helping with the harvest, and we had a horse called "Dirty Dick". Nobody thought to tell me that the horse was splay footed. As I turned him to the rick, he not only trod on my big toe (right foot) but turned on it too. All went quiet until some silly man asked "Did he hurt you?" I could barely speak but ground out "What do you think?" They helped me up onto the horse's back and sent me back to the house. Suddenly I was filled with rage and kicked the horse in its sides. It ran down that field as if it had Lester Piggott on its back. It was a very long field and we shot through the gate like a cannon ball, although he did stop at the house. I got a telling off for kicking him, but my reply was "You haven't got a toe that hurt like mine did".

It turned out that I had to have my foot seen to every six weeks. I lost the toe nail later, and it has never grown properly since. I have now forgiven "Dirty Dick", but at the time I could have killed him.'

Mrs M A Phipps

'We had a raw deal during the war. It was really an important job, keeping the country and two forces fed, and I can tell you it was hard work but I wouldn't have missed it.

I was at Keighley, York and Darfield, then I was sent to Oxfordshire. I was in three hostels up to the end of the war mixing with girls from all over the country, and what a time we had. We went to different farms most days. I can remember the farmer telling me to wash the cows' udders before milking, so I got a bucket of cold water, wrung the cloth and just slapped it on the cow's teats. The cow jumped two feet in the air, so the farmer said I had done it wrong; "Put your head on the cow's backend so that it gets used to your touch, then gently wash its teats. After all, you wouldn't like it" he said, laughing.

The best time was when we went out after work into Witney to the pub, then the G.I.s would rush in - to the locals they were loud and brash, but we loved it. That uniform and that aftershave ! "Gee, honey, where have you been all my life? You big, beautiful blonde". Corny, but we loved it. If the weather was cold, they would let us borrow their earmuffs when we were at work. The warden at the hostel would invite the G.I.s for a social evening - she liked to keep an eye on us. When they were shipped to France for the invasion it was awful; the place was so quiet. We just sat and cried; they were somebody's sons and I liked to think they enjoyed our company. After all, they were a long way from home. I remember this little song they used to sing in the pub.

> *"I don't want your green back dollars*
> *I don't want your watch and chain.*
> *All I want is you my darling,*
> *Darling please come back again".*

That's all I can remember. I can't listen to "I'll Be Seeing You" without having a little weep, thinking about my G.I. from Ohio.

Mrs Iris Petersen,

Bolton-on-Dearne, South Yorkshire

'I spent five years in the W.L.A., one year in North Devon from October 1944 to December 1945. I remember the G.I.s very well. I had a younger sister who used to find packets of sweets and gum on the doormat - it came through the letter box!

I can also remember going to the Catholic Service at the American camp on a Sunday with my Mother and sister. One Sunday morning, the G.I.s surrounded my Mother to shake her hand as it was their Mother's Day - I have never forgotten that.

The Catholic Padre used to come to our house for a bath and always left a bar of soap in the bathroom. We also had plenty of food parcels and Mum would cook a meal for some of the men. I believe it was 1943 when the G.I.s came to Devon to train for combat duties. At that time I worked for a Military School for young boys and, of course, the boys always asked if I could get them doughnuts!

Before I was called up I worked in the school hospital and one young G.I. used to give me doughnuts - he was called Kaplan. The message with the doughnuts was always:

> *"Doughnuts to you from all over the map;*
> *Doughnuts to you direct from Kap".*

I often wonder if he is still alive.'

Mrs Maureen Risbridges

'My friend Joan and I joined the W.L.A. in 1942 when we were seventeen. We were supposed to go to a hostel in Newgate, Pembrokeshire, but owing to heavy gales were transferred to Penty-y-Park near Haverfordwest, Wales.

Quite a lot of G.I.s were based near us and we knew a lot from the 75th Division. I always seemed to meet Bills, but I must say that they treated us with great respect, not like the ones who were stationed in Liverpool.

Sometimes we were put on Forestry and met the G.I.s living in the Welsh castles. In the dinner hour they had tinned peaches, etc, and invited us to tuck in, which we jolly well did. If we had a date at night we would work in our curlers, so that the first sight the G.I.s had of us was hard working prisoners (so they thought). Of course when they saw us in our uniform and civvies, and being able to come and go as we pleased, they realised their mistake. They would send huge lorries to take us to their parties where there would be wonderful great big cakes with 'Women's Land Army' on top, besides the A.T.S. and Airforce. It was nice to be mentioned for once. We were not always recognised as a fighting force and often got left out of things during the war. When we came out it was with an overcoat, a pair of shoes and one shirt (no gratuity for us).

At one point, we were transferred for a few weeks to Hodgesen Hill Hostel for potato picking as they were short handed. We were near the main road to Tenby, so would whistle at the trucks going past for lifts as we had to be in at 10.30 pm.

One American was sweet on me, but I didn't feel the same about him. If he couldn't track me down, he would follow my friends around. I think his name was Thomas, and if he caught me anywhere I used to fob him off with some tale that I made up on the spur of the moment. He just wouldn't take no for an answer. One night we were in the N.A.A.F.I. canteen and he came in pestering me, so I agreed to go out for a ride in the lorry if my friend came too. Riding merrily along he suddenly built up speed, then threatened to let go of the wheel if I didn't promise to make another date with him. I said No, and he promptly let go of the wheel. I grabbed it and hung on for dear life while my friends stuck their heads out of the window and screamed blue murder. How I did it I shall never know, for as we went round a corner there was a woman pushing a pram. I begged Thomas to take the wheel, promising to go out with him again, which I duly did one more time. He was a gentleman, but his goodnight kiss was awful for he had buck teeth. That was the end of that friendship. I guess he was moved on for I was never bothered again.

I would love to meet all my old pals who were in the Land Army with me. We had some great times even though the work was hard, but boy didn't we get brown. Writing this letter has brought it all back, and also the songs; "Stage Door Canteen" and "Paper Doll".

I left the W.L.A. in 1948 to get married to a German Prisoner of War. Sadly, I lost my husband in 1979.'

Mrs Schneiders
Merseyside

Spoon or spanner?

In old Civvy Street
I could bake quite a treat
In a truly professional manner.
But whilst there's a war,
I can't bake anymore;
'Cos I've now changed my spoon for a spanner.

Now my tarts could delight
They were awfully light
And my cakes - well, I dare bet a tanner
If it wasn't for Huns
They could beat anyones,
But I've now changed my spoon for a spanner.

If the war could be won
On just making a bun
I know I'd come home with a banner.
But instead I'll come back
Looking awfully black
With no spoon in my hand, but a spanner.

D Marshall 90223
Yorks N.R.

Chapter 3

HAPPY RECOLLECTIONS OF THE G.I.s

'I was at Filxton Airbase in England, 1944.

I met a few of the Land Girls at the dances I went to on our base. The girls I met were very nice and hard worked, from what they told me they were doing for their country.

I thought that it was great of the girls to take the time out to come to the dances and make us G.I.s feel at home. Although it is now 50 years ago, I still remember how good it was to talk to a girl for a change, instead of another G.I.

I think that it is great that someone at last is taking up the Land Girl's case. The W.L.A. should have their day of "Honour" and recognition for all that they did for their country when it was needed.'

Rocco P Lotesto
Crestwood, U.S.A.

'My name is Tony Stirpe and I was with 1260th M P Company attached to the 357th Fighter Group. I arrived in England on October 20th 1943 and moved to our based in Leiston on or about November 15th, 1943.

First, I must tell you that I met Connie Ward, who was with the Women's Land Army stationed in Leiston, on one Sunday afternoon on November 27th, 1943, whilst I was guard at the main gate. We started dating the following week. I became very friendly with most of the 30 girls that were at the Hostel. They were all girls aged 18 to 20 and very new to farm life.

On my pass days, I would go to the farms that Connie would be working at and watch them doing their farm duties. Connie and a Maude Brown were assigned to an old Steam Run Thrashing Machine. They did a man's job. I find that they deserve all the credit of everyone they replaced for the war effort.

Connie and I dated for about 2 years and were married on February 11th 1945. Connie stayed in the Land Army until April 21st 1945.

Now I must tell you a little about Connie. In September 1943, she had her choice of the branch of the service she wanted to be in. She chose the Land Army thinking she would be stationed near her home in Leeds. She boarded a train in Leeds with six other girls and they were on their way to Leiston. None of these girls had ever heard of Leiston, so that was already a disappointment to them . These girls were all

18 years old and still green, not being away before. This was a first for Connie. It was the best thing that happened to me. We were married at the Church of the Holy Souls, Carr Avenue, Leiston. Now we have been married 46 years and have a happy life. We have one son who is married and has three children, we have had a good, full life.

My wife and I have visited England many times. She still has a family in Leeds, and we plan to visit again.

Connie's address at the Land Army was Connie Ward, W.L.A. Hostel, The White Horse, Leiston. Our Maid of Honour was Gladys Kirk, who lives near Wakefield.

There were 30 girls at the Hostel, with a Mr and Mrs Hodges in charge. The girls had strict rules to obey. They had a 10.00 pm curfew and if they were one minute late, the door was locked; then they had to knock to get in. There was no excuse that you could give Mrs Hodges. She just enforced the curfew and they were punished - maybe for one day without leaving the Hostel.

CONNIE WARD AND TONY STIRPE MARRY AT THE CHURCH OF THE HOLY SOULS, CARR AVE, LEISTON, FEBRUARY 11TH 1945

MR & MRS TONY STIRPE WITH MEMBERS OF THE W.L.A. AND G.Is

A date with a girl in the Hostel was maybe a movie or a Saturday night dance and a stop at Testoni's Fish and Chip shop for our favourite 'Fish and Chips'.

The girls were paid 25 shillings a week for their service. In my opinion, the girls were all hard working and I was proud to know the girls at Leiston.

I can remember that when my wife was discharged from the Land Army, she was sent a letter requesting that she return her uniforms and work clothes - all she was able to keep was a necktie.

During the war everything in England was rationed, including shoes and clothing. When my wife went to buy her wedding gown, she had to use all her clothing coupons that were allotted to her for the year.

When we were married, we had a reception after the ceremony at the Hotel with all the Land Army girls. After the reception, we boarded a train in Leiston for London where we had a wonderful honeymoon; even though there were the V2 rockets bombing London, we were able to enjoy ourselves.

I am enclosing a copy of the Hotel statement of what our charges were in 1945 - ours was the bridal suite. Today the same suite would be over £100 a day.

I like your title - it fits the girls perfectly!'

Tony Stirpe, Lyons
New York, U.S.A.

No. 104

Cpl. & Mrs. Stirpe

TELEPHONE: FROBISHER 8131
TELEGRAMS: "BAILEY'S HOTEL, LONDON."

**BAILEY'S HOTEL,
LONDON, S.W.7.**

February 1945	11			12			13			14			15								
	£	s.	d.	£	s.	d.	£	s.	d.	£	s.	d.	£	s.	d.	£	s.	d.		s.	d
Brought forward				2	6		4	6	5	6	14	2	8	7	5						
Apartments & Bfst	1	10	–	1	10		1	10	–	1	10										
Service (To Rooms)																					
Inclusive Terms																					
Breakfast																					
Luncheon																					
Dinner		10			5			10													
Afternoon Tea																					
Tea and Coffee																					
Supper																					
Children's Board																					
Servant's „																					
Wines																					
Liqueurs and Spirits																					
Ales and Stout								1	7												
Mineral Waters					9																
Sandwiches																					
Dessert																					
Fires																					
SERVICE CHARGE 10%		4			3	8		4	2		3										
and Cigarettes																					
Hire																					
ibus											3										
Theatre Tickets																					
House Chs.		2			1			2													
Total	2	6		4	6	5	6	14	2	8	7	5									
Less Paid																					
Carried forward																					

NOT subject to Service charge

PLEASE LEAVE KEY AT OFFICE

S&P 13736 Visitors are kindly requested to advise the Proprietors of any complaints to the Head Office—35 New Bridge Street, London, E.C.4

BAILEY'S HOTEL BILL

WOMEN'S LAND ARMY

East Suffolk County Office

Telephone:
Ipswich 4413/4.   71,St.Matthew's Street,
Ref:MG/GT.   Ipswich.
                              19th April,1945.

Mrs.M.Stirpe,
W.L.A.Hostel,
The White Horse,
LEISTON.

Dear Mrs.Stirpe,

I enclose herewith your official release from the Land Army, dated Saturday next - 21st April- and I will ask my Uniform Department to get into touch with you with regard to the return of your Uniform.

I should like to thank you for the work which you have put in for the Land Army during the past year and eight months, and to wish you every happiness in your married life.

Yours sincerely,
pp Ethel Sunderland Taylor

Organising Secretary.

Ministry of Agriculture and Fisheries

WOMEN'S LAND ARMY

Volunteer No. W.L.A.: 133076.

Mrs.:   STIRPE, M.
Miss

Home Address: 32,Ney Street,
                       Green Road,
                       LEEDS, 9.

has been discharged from the Women's Land Army after 1 year & 8 months' service.

Signed: pp Ethel Sunderland Taylor

County Secretary for East Suffolk.

Address: 71, St. Matthew's Street,Ipswich.

Date of discharge: 21st April,1945.

WOMEN'S LAND ARMY - EAST SUFFOLK COUNTY OFFICE RELEASE LETTER

MINISTRY OF AGRICULTURE AND FISHERIES DISCHARGE LETTER

'I had dealings with Land Army girls.

I, for one, am very glad there were such people. I knew several of them and they seemed to be hard working girls who were taking the place of the men who were the farm workers, but were at that time in uniform.

I met Audrey Clegg at the dance hall in Saxmundham, a small town outside our base in Leiston, Suffolk. Dances were held there every Wednesday and Saturday nights, and I was there every night I could make it.

Audrey loved to dance and I did too. We were not drinkers so we did not go to the local pub, but we did go to the Fish and Chip shop. I would ride my bike to Middleton where Audrey was billeted and we would bike to Saxmundham to dance.

Audrey's parents lived in Beeston, a small town outside Nottingham. I met her parents several times when I was on a 2-day pass.

Audrey worked on a farm in the town of Middleton and did most of the jobs the men had to do. The job she liked best was milking the cows twice a day!!

These girls worked very hard and their effort to help win the war cannot be measured. I asked Audrey to marry me and she agreed, but we decided to wait until the war was over.

In 1947, Audrey arrived in the United States and we were married. Since then we have had 6 children, 3 boys and 3 girls. We now have 7 grandchildren and after 45 years of happiness, we are still going strong.

As far as the Land Girls are concerned, to me they were the GREATEST.'

Pat Buzzeo
Boynton Beach, U.S.A

'Your book "Land Army Days" sure is a good subject to write about.

As we served in World War II in Suffolk County at the Leiston Air Base, we witnessed the hardships of the English people at that time and as the G.I.s we became friends with many of them; friendships that in some instances continue today.

As U.S. military men, most of us had very little connection with any of the various branches of the British military. We respected them, for they were into the battle before we were and the hardships for them were many.

Back in those days, the 357th Fighter Group had

no ladies serving in our U.S. military except for a few American Red Cross girls serving at our canteen. One certainly had to admire the ladies in any branch of the British military, for they served their country well.

The Land Army girls performed the work of men as they replaced them on the farms where the men had been called up.

I had been married five years prior to entering the U.S. military, so I behaved myself. I had a best war buddy who did "get about", who is now deceased. I recall on Wednesday nights, there was G.I. truck that transported G.I.s to Ipswich where there was dancing with English gals, mostly of the military. I went there once with my friend. The music was great and the gals were good dancers but to be there made me "home-sick" so I never went again.

My friend did become friendly with persons at the Ipswich Canteen or Red Cross Club. He met one gal whose home was at Yoxford near our Leiston airbase. One Sunday, my friend, this Army gal and I, as well as another Army gal, were released from duty and the gal's widowed mother invited us to her home for a chicken dinner. It made a nice day for all of us. I am fairly sure the gal's name was Connie Bradbury. My friend used to take his laundry to the widow Bradbury.

Our mode of travel was via the English bicycles that were issued to us at the base.

For years, I have served as Corresponding Secretary for the 357th Fighter Group Association. We have a mailing list of about 500 members including about 60 Associate members. Most of our Associate members are widows of our deceased members. Within this group of members, several married English girls as the war came to a close. My wife and I are friendly with these girls and they are all fine people.'

Joe De Shay
Boca Raton, U.S.A

'**H**ello!

Once upon a time, one hundred years ago or so it seems, I met one of the most beautiful girls I have ever known in my life, and believe me, I have known some lovely girls in my time!

This stunning female was a member of the Womens Land Army and she and her mates were working the fields south of Croydon in the area between where we were billeted (Sipson College) and the Airfield where we worked (Heston Aerodrome). I recall that area well. All the "Buzz Bombs" that overshot London landed in or around Croydon!!

This young woman was about 20, I would guess.

HAPPY RECOLLECTIONS OF THE G.I.s

Lovely blonde hair, blue eyes and a body straight out of Heaven, but for the life of me I cannot remember her name. Impeccable manners and worlds of class. I was captivated from the first day. Madly in love (?) - at 23, I'm not sure you really know.

We dated. We danced. We "smooched". She made the rules. Sexual intercourse was completely out of the picture and this was made clear on the second or third date when she informed me she was engaged to a young RAF man taking pilot training in the States.

This lovely affair lasted until I was posted to Biggin Hill at Bromley and the last time I saw her was when we "buzzed" the field where she was working, upon her request. We flew so low over that field that I could look into her face from the cockpit window. She blew me a kiss! Wonderful memories.

ERNEST P. MORGAN - AERIAL GUNNER 1949 ONE OF MANY G.I.s WHO REMEMBERS WITH DEEP RESPECT AND AFFECTION ALL MEMBERS OF THAT MIGHTY BAND OF GIRLS -"THE WOMEN'S LAND ARMY".

I have known some of these young ladies in the W.L.A. to be so tired and worn out in the evenings after work they cried, yet they had so high a regard for their duties they would never allow an outsider to demean or talk down on their assignment.

It is a real shame and disgrace to learn now that these tried and true loyalties have been discarded like an old shoe! Is it a case of Britain being too proud to admit that pretty little girls from all walks of life put together a work force second to none and got the job done?

Forgive me if I go overboard on this thing. It's just that I do remember that lovely, sweet young blonde headed girl with more class in her little finger than most people acquire in a lifetime who came from one of the office complexes of a very large London firm to dig in the dirt of farmlands and shrugged her shoulders and smiled when you questioned the logic of such a move. It was a duty to be done, she would say, and that was that.

From all of us ex G.I.s - we love your country and you!!'

Ernie Morgan
Stone Mountain, G.A., U.S.A